유희태 일반영어 ② 유형

LSI 영어연구소 유희태 박사 저

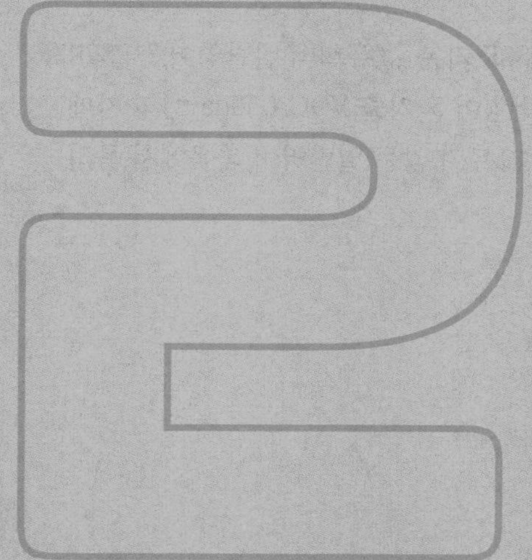

PREFACE

《2S2R 유형》은 2014년 초판이 출간된 후, 1년 후인 2015년에 개정판, 2017년에 3판, 2020년에 4판, 이번에 5판이 나왔다. 이번 5판은 4판이 가지고 있는 여러 가지 한계를 극복하기 위해 출간되었다. 노량진에서 강의하면서 4판의 장점과 단점에 대해 수험생들과 의견을 교환할 많은 기회가 있었다. 이 5판은 그 대화의 산물이다.

이 5판 교재는 2S2R 방법론의 구체화라는 지향점을 가졌던 4판과 형식적으로 큰 변화는 없다. 이전 판본들이 단순히 문제를 푸는 것에 집중되어 있었다면, 4판과 5판은 《2S2R 기본》에서 배운 2S2R 방법론을 더욱 심화할 수 있어서 학습의 연속성 측면에서 장점이 있다고 할 수 있다. 하지만 이번 5판은 4판과 차이점이 있는데, 우선, 양적인 측면에서 4판의 분량이 너무 많아 학습하기가 부담스럽다는 수험생들의 의견이 꽤 있었기 때문에 500페이지 넘는 분량을 이번 교재에서는 10% 정도 감축하였다. 또한, 4판에 있는 몇몇 문제들의 정답이 애매한 경우도 있었고, 오타도 있었다. 이번 5판은 이런 오류들을 모두 잡았고, 분석에 어울리지 않는 지문들도 제외했다.

《유희태 일반영어 2-2S2R 유형》은 《유희태 일반영어 1-2S2R 기본》, 《유희태 일반영어 3-2S2R 기출》, 《유희태 일반영어 4-2S2R 문제은행》, 《유희태 일반영어 5-기출 VOCA 30days》의 자매편이다. 모든 시리즈를 체계적으로 공부한다면 점수가 잘 오르지 않는 일반영어 과목에서 목적한 바의 성취를 충분히 얻을 것이다.

《유희태 일반영어》 시리즈를 효과적으로 활용하는 방법은, 대학 1학년 때 《2S2R 기본》을 최소 3회독, 평균 5회독하여 일반영어 기본 이론을 확실하게 다진 뒤, 2학년 때 《2S2R 유형》을 최소 3회독하여 임용 유형에 기본 이론을 확장 적용하는 훈련을 하고, 3학년 때 《2S2R 기출》을 2회독한 다음, 처음으로 치르는 4학년 때 《2S2R 문제은행》을 가지고 공부하는 것이다. 이 과정에서 《기출 VOCA 30days》는 1학년 때부터 주 6회 매일 20분씩 꾸준히 공부하기를 추천한다.

이 5판을 출간하는 데 많은 분들의 도움을 받았다. 출간하는 과정에서 여러 조언과 지원을 아끼지 않았던 박문각의 변수경 님, 또한 교정 작업과 번역작업에서 도움을 준 LSI 영어연구소 소속의 Sean Maylone 수석연구원과 연구실 조교들에게도 고마움을 전한다. 아무쪼록 이 교재가 수험생 여러분의 합격에 일조하기를 기대한다.

2021년 12월 LSI 영어연구소에서

유희태

CONTENTS

Part 01
기입형

Chapter 01 요지, 목적찾기 8

Chapter 02 제목찾기 26

Chapter 03 빈칸추론 38

Chapter 04 지칭추론 80

서술형

Chapter 01 의미찾기 100

Chapter 02 함축의미, 추론 154

Chapter 03 요지, 목적, 제목 170

Chapter 04 지칭추론 184

유희태 일반영어 ②

2S2R

유형

_Part

01

기입형

CHAPTER

01 요지, 목적찾기

모범답안 및 번역 p.006

01 **Read the passage and follow the directions.** [2 points]

Ben Yannick stands 6 feet, 7 inches tall. His height makes him especially self-conscious at scientific conferences when he rises to describe his research as a demographer at the London School of Tropical Medicine. “It’s always quite embarrassing,” he said.

Dr. Yannick, who is Dutch, studies why his fellow citizens are so tall. Today, the Dutch are on average the tallest people on the planet. Just 150 years ago, they were relatively short. In 1860, the average Dutch soldier in the Netherlands was just 5 feet 5 inches. American men were 2.7 inches taller. Since 1860, average heights have increased in many parts of the world, but no people have shot up like the Dutch. The average Dutchman now stands over six feet tall. And while the growth spurt in the United States has stopped in recent years, the Dutch continue to get taller.

For years, scientists have sought to understand why average height has increased, and why the Dutch in particular have grown so quickly. Among other factors, the Dutch have a better diet than in the past, and they also have better medical care. But now Dr. Yannick has found evidence suggesting that evolution is also helping to make them taller.

The new study was made possible thanks to a major medical database recently established in the Netherlands called LifeLines. The database contains a vast amount of information, including genetic profiles and medical records, about tens of thousands of Dutch families. Dr. Yannick analyzed data on 42,612 men and women over age 45, looking at the height of their subjects and how many children they had. Dutch men who were taller than average had more children than those of average or lower than average height. Among those born in the early 1950s, for example, men who were 5 feet 6 inches had on average 2.15 children. Men who were 6 feet 1 inch had 2.39 children. The trend toward taller men having more children persisted for more than 35 years. Under identical conditions, some people will grow taller than others because they carry certain genetic variations.

What is the main argument put forward by Dr. Yannick in the passage? Write your answer by filling in each blank below with ONE word from the passage. The first word should be capitalized.

______①______ helps to give an account of Dutch ______②______ advantage.

NOTE

Step 1	Survey
Key Words	
Signal Words	
Step 2	**Reading**
Purpose	
Pattern of Organization	
Tone	
Main Idea	
Step 3	**Summary**
지문 요약하기 (Paraphrasing)	
Step 4	**Recite**
	요약문 말로 설명하기

02 **Read the passage and follow the directions.** [2 points]

The sailors who threw Jonah overboard imagined his presence to be the cause of the storm which threatened to wreck their ship. In a similar spirit the Japanese, at the time of the Tokyo earthquake took to massacring Koreans and Liberals. When the Romans won victories in the Punic wars, the Carthaginians became persuaded that their misfortunes were due to a certain laxity which had crept into the worship of Moloch. Moloch liked having children sacrificed to him, and preferred them aristocratic; but the noble families of Carthage had adopted the practice of surreptitiously substituting plebeian children for their own offspring. This, it was thought, had displeased the god, and at the worst moments even the most aristocratic children were duly consumed in the fire. Strange to say, the Romans were victorious in spite of this democratic reform on the part of their enemies. Collective fear stimulates herd instinct, and tends to produce ferocity toward those who are not regarded as members of the herd. So it was in the French Revolution, when dread of foreign armies produced the reign of terror. And it is to be feared that the Nazis, as defeat draws nearer, will increase the intensity of their campaign for exterminating Jews. Neither a man nor a crowd nor a nation can be trusted to act humanely or to think sanely under the influence of the irrational emotion. And for this reason poltroons are more prone to cruelty than brave men, and are also more prone to superstition. When I say this, I am thinking of men who are brave in all respects, not only in facing death. Many a man will have the courage to die gallantly, but will not have the courage to say, or even to think, that the cause for which he is asked to die is an unworthy one.

What is the main idea of the passage? Write your answer by filling in each blank below with ONE word from the passage respectively.

Terror generates impulses of ____①____, and therefore promotes ____②____ beliefs as seem to justify it. Courageous men are less liable to cruelty than ____③____.

NOTE

Step 1	Survey
Key Words	
Signal Words	
Step 2	**Reading**
Purpose	
Pattern of Organization	
Tone	
Main Idea	
Step 3	**Summary**
지문 요약하기 (Paraphrasing)	
Step 4	**Recite**
요약문 말로 설명하기	

03 **Read the passage and follow the directions.** [2 points]

To understand why the National Rifle Association and fellow pro-gun groups have been so successful in stopping gun control legislation, consider the dilemma that faced the former senator Mark Begich, an Alaskan Democrat in April 2013, when the Senate was voting on expanding background checks after the Newtown shooting. Begich was up for re-election in 2014. He knew that many Alaskans were gun owners, and many gun owners are single-issue gun voters. He also knew that while other Alaskans may want tougher gun control, most of these were probably Democrats, who'd support him anyway. And so, along fellow Democrats in gun-dense states like Arkansas, North Dakota and Montana, Begich made the rational political calculus. He voted against gun control, and then lost anyway.

The National Rifle Association poses a credible threat to any lawmaker who crosses it. It uses a clear rating system to evaluate candidates. It helps its 3 million members broadcast their demands. Many will support candidates based on N.R.A. ratings alone. The N.R.A. also spends aggressively in congressional races($28.4 million in outside expenditures in 2014), and can deliver votes, which is even more valuable than money. By contrast, groups that support gun control legislation haven't yet proved they can deliver enough single-issue voters to decide a close election. While these groups are growing in size and membership, they still have a long way to go.

The gun lobby also benefits from geography, particularly in the Senate. Low-population states are more likely to be heavy gun-owning states, and low-population states have disproportionate influence in the Senate. In the House, gun control-supporting Democrats disproportionately concentrate in safe-seat urban districts and swing districts are mostly rural or suburban, and home to higher concentrations of pro-gun voters. For even modest gun control legislation to pass, majorities in both chambers must be convinced that the political cost of opposing gun control is higher than the political cost of crossing the gun lobby.

What is the main idea of the passage? Write your answer by filling in each blank with appropriate ONE or TWO word(s) from the passage.

Gun lobby has passion, money, and ____ⓐ____. No mass shooting will change the politics of gun reform until a(n) ____ⓑ____ group can match the organized power of the gun lobby.

NOTE

Step 1	Survey
Key Words	
Signal Words	
Step 2	**Reading**
Purpose	
Pattern of Organization	
Tone	
Main Idea	
Step 3	**Summary**
지문 요약하기 (Paraphrasing)	
Step 4	**Recite**
요약문 말로 설명하기	

04 **Read the passage and follow the directions.** [2 points]

The acid that carries genetic information in every human cell, DNA, contains just four chemicals: adenine, cytosine, guanine, and thymine. But a single gene is "spelled out" by perhaps a million combinations. As the Human Genome Project (which provided a "map" of human genes) was nearing completion in the spring of 2000, there were a number of newspaper headlines about specific discoveries: "Gene Linked to Anxiety." "Gay Gene!" and "Thrill Seeking Due to Genetics." The newspaper articles led people to believe that a single gene is responsible for a certain personality trait, in the same way a single gene can be responsible for a physical characteristic or disease. However, one gene alone cannot cause people to become anxious, homosexual or thrill-seeking. Instead, many genes work together, and they do direct the combination of chemicals in the body. These chemicals, such as dopamine and serotonin (which affect a person's mood) have a significant influence on personality.

What is the main idea of the passage? Write your answer by filling in each blank below with the ONE most appropriate word. The first word should be capitalized.

______ⓐ______ is influenced by the combination of many ______ⓑ______.

____

____

NOTE

Step 1	Survey
Key Words	
Signal Words	
Step 2	**Reading**
Purpose	
Pattern of Organization	
Tone	
Main Idea	
Step 3	**Summary**
지문 요약하기 (Paraphrasing)	
Step 4	**Recite**
요약문 말로 설명하기	

05 **Read the passage and follow the directions.** [4 points]

Like most of my generation, I was brought up on the saying: "Satan finds some mischief for idle hands to do." Being a highly virtuous child, I believed all that I was told, and acquired a conscience which has kept me working hard down to the present moment. But although my conscience has controlled my actions, my opinions have undergone a revolution. I think that there is far too much work done in the world and that what needs to be preached in modern industrial countries is quite different from what always has been preached. Everyone knows the story of the traveler in Naples who saw twelve beggars lying in the sun (it was before the days of Mussolini), and offered a lira to the idlest of them. Eleven of them jumped up to claim it, so he gave it to the twelfth. This traveler was on the right lines. But in countries which do not enjoy Mediterranean sunshine ____①____ is more difficult, and a great public propaganda will be required to inaugurate it. I hope that the leaders of the YMCA will start a campaign to induce good young men to do nothing. If so, I shall not have lived in vain.

Complete the idea that the writer is conveying by filling in the blank with ONE word from the passage. Second, fill in the blank with the ONE most appropriate word from the passage. If necessary, change the word form.

Immense harm is caused by the belief that much work is ____②____.

NOTE

Step 1	Survey
Key Words	
Signal Words	
Step 2	**Reading**
Purpose	
Pattern of Organization	
Tone	
Main Idea	
Step 3	**Summary**
지문 요약하기 (Paraphrasing)	
Step 4	**Recite**
요약문 말로 설명하기	

06 **Read the passage and follow the directions.** [2 points]

American consumers are addicted to water. The average American uses over 2,000 gallons of water each day—two times the global average. But only a fraction of this water use comes directly from the tap. Most of the water is consumed indirectly, having been funneled into agriculture or commercial production. This "water footprint" concept—which accounts for the total volume of freshwater used to produce the goods and services we consume—is the most holistic way to look at our water use and is an important tool for identifying wasteful practices. An incredible 40 percent of the water consumed by Americans goes into meat and dairy production. Livestock must drink water and there is some water use at the farm, but most of this water is used for producing animal feed. Furthermore, a quarter of the water used in the U.S., including water that is polluted in the process, goes toward producing commodities for export. The water challenge is also huge worldwide. To ensure that the water footprint of humanity will not grow, given projected population growth, the average water footprint per capita will have to decrease significantly. Improved technologies alone will not be sufficient to achieve the required water footprint reduction. The unhealthy U.S. consumption pattern needs to be reconsidered. Taking shorter showers will not suffice. Eating less meat—the biggest water user in the diet—would be much more effective.

Complete the idea that the writer is conveying by filling in the blank ⓐ with ONE word from the passage and ⓑ with TWO consecutive words from the passage respectively.

In order to save ____ⓐ____, we have to change our ____ⓑ____.

NOTE

Step 1	Survey
Key Words	
Signal Words	
Step 2	**Reading**
Purpose	
Pattern of Organization	
Tone	
Main Idea	
Step 3	**Summary**
지문 요약하기 (Paraphrasing)	
Step 4	**Recite**
요약문 말로 설명하기	

07 **Read the passage and follow the directions.** [2 points]

Not long ago, on the South Pacific islands of Micronesia, a seventeen-year-old boy named Sima got into an argument with his father. He was staying with his family at his grandfather's house when his father-a stern and demanding man-ordered him out of bed early one morning and told him to find a bamboo pole-knife to harvest breadfruit. Sima spent hours in the village, looking without success for a pole-knife, and when he returned empty-handed, his father was furious. The family would now go hungry, he told his son, waving a machete in rage. "Get out of here and go find somewhere else to live."

Sima left his grandfather's house and walked back to his home village. Along the way he ran into his fourteen-year-old brother and borrowed a pen. Two hours later, curious about where Sima had gone, his brother went looking for him. He returned to the now empty family house and peered in the window. In the middle of a dark room, hanging slack and still from a noose, was Sima. He was dead.

In the early 1960s, suicide among adolescence on the islands of Micronesia was almost unknown. But for reasons no one quite understands, it then began to rise, steeply and dramatically, by leaps and bounds every year, until by the end of the 1980s there were more suicides per capita in Micronesia than anywhere else in the world. For males between fifteen and twenty-four, the suicide rate in the United States is about 22 per 100,000. In the islands of Micronesia the rate is about 160 per 100,000—more than seven times higher. At that level, suicide is almost commonplace, triggered by the smallest of incidents. Sima took his own life because his father yelled at him. In the midst of the Micronesian epidemic, that was hardly unusual. Teens committed suicide on the islands because they saw their girlfriends with another boy, or because their parents refused to give them a few extra dollars for beer. One nineteen-year-old hanged himself because his parents didn't buy him a graduation gown. One seventeen-year-old hanged himself because he had been rebuked by his older brother for making too much noise.

Complete the idea that the writer is conveying in the passage by filling in each blank with the ONE most appropriate word from the passage. The first word should be capitalized.

______①______ is rare and pathological in western cultures, but it has become a ritual of ______②______ in Micronesia.

NOTE

Step 1	Survey
Key Words	
Signal Words	
Step 2	**Reading**
Purpose	
Pattern of Organization	
Tone	
Main Idea	
Step 3	**Summary**
지문 요약하기 (Paraphrasing)	
Step 4	**Recite**
요약문 말로 설명하기	

08 **Read the passage and follow the directions.** [2 points]

Watching the middle-aged Jimmy Connors defeat the middle-aged Martina Navratilova at Las Vegas, was not so much a tennis match as a fracas in the sex war. The 14,000 audience was split along gender lines with each victorious shot being acclaimed as proof of either male superiority or female equality. In the end, even though Connors was handicapped by having only one ball to serve and a 3ft wider court to receive in, he walked off with $500,000 prize money by vindicating the obvious: that at the top level of tennis men are faster and more powerful than women. Feminists have only God to blame for this unfairness.

Historically, women as yet have been no match for men in creative, imaginative or cultural endeavor. Although for almost 100 years they have not been seriously debarred from such activities in Western societies their achievements have been well below the standard of genius reached by men. Among the world's poets, no woman can be named confidently as ranking with the best. There has been no great woman composer. Nor a great woman philosopher. Even in painting, where one might have expected evidence of equal creative ability, there is only a sprinkling of women to be found in the influential movements of Impressionism, Fauvism, Surrealism, Cubism and Abstract Expressionism.

Resentment against male domination was voiced by newsreader Anna Ford, who complained that during the general election campaign no women at the BBC were given the job of doing serious interviews with top politicians. "We might have put different questions from those of the middle-aged, middle-class, white, Anglo-Saxon, Protestant men," she said. It is no good Anna Ford claiming that women might have different questions to ask. Indeed, they might, but who, bar a tiny majority, would want to hear the answers?

Describe the main idea that the writer is conveying in the passage by filling in each blank with ONE word from the passage respectively. If necessary, change the word form.

The assertion that women deserve ____ⓐ____ representation in every form of social activity, regardless of ability to match their male equivalents displays a preposterous disregard for the natural differences between the ____ⓑ____.

NOTE

Step 1	Survey
Key Words	
Signal Words	
Step 2	**Reading**
Purpose	
Pattern of Organization	
Tone	
Main Idea	
Step 3	**Summary**
지문 요약하기 (Paraphrasing)	
Step 4	**Recite**
요약문 말로 설명하기	

09 **Read the passage and follow the directions.** [2 points]

The concept of two warring souls within the body of the Black American was as meaningful for Du Bois at the end of his years as editor of *Crisis*, the official journal of the National Association for the Advancement of Colored People (NAACP), as when he had first used the image at the start of the century. The tension between race pride and identification with the nation as a whole was nowhere more dramatic than in the most controversial editorial ever printed in *Crisis*, "Close Ranks," which in July 1918 called on Black Americans to "forget our special grievances and close our ranks" with the White people "fighting for democracy" during the First World War. Bitterly criticized by Black people, Du Bois barely modified his statement when, two months later, he set the priorities for his readers: "first your Country, then your Rights!" Perhaps the editor had written more than he intended in using the word "forget," for *Crisis* before and after the editorial showed no diminution in its criticism of racism. But he distinguished between Allied and German ambitions, and declared that defeat of the former would be disastrous for that "United States of the World" to which he was most loyal. Du Bois nevertheless saw danger in the negation of race pride, by those who did not recognize their own beauty as Black people, for example. The responsibility of *Crisis* was to arbitrate between those who advocated race pride and those who denied any differences between the races. The focal point of the magazine's efforts in this respect came with the rise of Marcus Garvey, the gifted Jamaican leader whose "back-to-Africa" movement, as it was popularly called, was founded on the premise, according to Du Bois, that "a black skin was in itself a sort of patent to nobility."

What is the purpose of the passage? Write your answer by filling in each blank below with ONE or TWO word(s) from the passage.

It is to describe Du Bois's stance regarding Black American's ____①____ and ____②____ with the nation.

NOTE

Step 1	Survey
Key Words	
Signal Words	
Step 2	**Reading**
Purpose	
Pattern of Organization	
Tone	
Main Idea	
Step 3	**Summary**
지문 요약하기 (Paraphrasing)	
Step 4	**Recite**
요약문 말로 설명하기	

CHAPTER

02 제목찾기

모범답안 및 번역 p.024

01 **Read the passage and follow the directions.** [2 points]

Meditation is not an escape from daily living, but a preparation for it, and what is of surpassing importance is what we bring back from the experience. Like pearl divers, meditators plunge deep into the inner ocean of consciousness and hope to come swimming back to the surface with jewels of great price.

At the most modest level, by providing a way of staying with an issue long enough to turn all its facets to the light, meditation can help solve day-to-day problems. One man, burdened with a periodically insane wife and three troubled adolescent children, told me that his only cure, when difficulties get too pressing, is to take out his sailboat. Outbound, he said, "I don't think about my problems. I concentrate on the sun on the water; I watch the sails bending in the wind. Sometimes I think about all the other men who have to put out to sea, and I wonder what they thought about. By the time I am inbound my mind is calm. Then I begin to see things as they really are and find I can deal with them."

If meditation accomplishes no more than that, it has done a great deal. Psychoanalyst Erich Fromm, after addressing a Canadian audience, was asked for "a practical solution to the problems of living." "Quietness" Fromm replied at once. "The experience of stillness. You have to stop in order to be able to change direction."

Complete the title of the passage by filling in the blank with ONE word from the passage.

____①____ as an Effective Answer to ____②____.

NOTE

Step 1	Survey
Key Words	
Signal Words	
Step 2	**Reading**
Purpose	
Pattern of Organization	
Tone	
Main Idea	
Step 3	**Summary**
지문 요약하기 (Paraphrasing)	
Step 4	**Recite**
요약문 말로 설명하기	

02 **Read the passage and follow the directions.** [2 points]

Democritus, a Greek philosopher, said that all atoms are small, hard particles. He thought that atoms were made of a single material formed into different shapes and sizes. The word "atom" is derived from the Greek word "atomos" which means "not able to be divided." In 1803, John Dalton, a school teacher, proposed his atomic theory. Dalton's theory states that elements (substances composed of only one type of atom) combine in certain proportions to form compounds. In 1897, a British scientist named J. J. Thomson experimented with a cathode-ray tube which had a positively charged plate. The plate attracted negatively charged particles that we now call electrons. Rather than being indivisible particles, Thomson's plum-pudding atomic model states that atoms contain negatively charged electrons embedded within a sea of positive charge. In 1909, Ernest Rutherford conducted an experiment in which he aimed a beam of positively charged particles at a thin sheet of gold foil. Most of the particles went straight through the gold foil, some were deflected and others bounced straight back. Because some of the particles bounced straight back, Rutherford was able to show that the center of the atom, the nucleus, is positively charged and very small. The nucleus contains protons, which are positively charged, and neutrons, which are neutral. In 1913, Niels Bohr, a Danish scientist who worked with Dr. Rutherford, proposed that electrons move around the nucleus in certain paths, or energy levels. This model was improved upon by an Austrian physicist named Erwin Schröedinger and a German physicist named Werner Heisenberg. Schröedinger and Heisenberg proposed that electrons do not move in definite paths around the nucleus, but are found in regions around the nucleus called electron clouds.

What is the title of the passage? Write your answer by filling in the blank with TWO consecutive words from the passage.

The History of the ______________________.

NOTE

Step 1	Survey
Key Words	
Signal Words	
Step 2	**Reading**
Purpose	
Pattern of Organization	
Tone	
Main Idea	
Step 3	**Summary**
지문 요약하기 (Paraphrasing)	
Step 4	**Recite**
요약문 말로 설명하기	

03 **Read the passage and follow the directions.** [2 points]

Nevada began its transition to a modern economy during the Great Depression of the 1930s. After the legalization of gambling in 1931 and the reduction to six weeks of the residence requirement for divorce, Nevada became a marriage, divorce, and resort center. The principal resort areas are Las Vegas, Reno, Laughlin, and Lake Tahoe. Las Vegas attracts many tourists from southern California and foreign countries and also hosts business and professional conventions. Reno draws many pleasure seekers from the San Francisco Bay area and from the Pacific Northwest. Laughlin emerged as a tourist center in the 1980s, and Lake Tahoe continues to serve as a fashionable playground. Construction of the Hoover Dam on the Colorado River substantially aided the economy of southern Nevada, and its cheap hydroelectric power opened the way for manufacturing. The importation of both hydroelectric power from the Bonneville Dam on the Columbia River and piped-in natural gas brought industrial development to the northwestern region.

What is the title of the passage? Write your answer by filling in the blank with below with TWO consecutive words from the passage.

The Creation of a(n) ______________________ in Nevada.

NOTE

Step 1	Survey
Key Words	
Signal Words	
Step 2	**Reading**
Purpose	
Pattern of Organization	
Tone	
Main Idea	
Step 3	**Summary**
지문 요약하기 (Paraphrasing)	
Step 4	**Recite**
요약문 말로 설명하기	

04 **Read the passage and follow the directions.** [2 points]

The general key to effective listening in interpersonal situations is to listen actively. Perhaps the best preparation for active listening is to act physically and mentally like an alert listener. For many people, this may be the most abused rule of effective listening. Recall, for example, how your body almost automatically reacts to important news: Almost immediately, you assume an upright posture and remain relatively still and quiet. You do this almost reflexively because this is the way you listen most effectively. Even more important than this ______①______ alertness is mental alertness. As a listener, participate in the communication as an equal partner with the speaker, as one who is emotionally and intellectually ready to engage in the sharing of meaning. Active listening is expressive. Let the speaker know that you are participating in the communication process. Nonverbally, maintain eye contact, focus your concentration on the speaker rather than on others present, and express your feeling facially. Verbally, ask appropriate questions, signal understanding with "I see" or "yes," and express agreement or disagreement as appropriate.

Passive listening is, however, not without merit. Passive listening—listening without talking or directing the speaker in any obvious way—is a powerful means of communicating acceptance. This is the kind of listening that people ask for when they say, "Just listen to me." They are essentially asking you to suspend your judgment and "just listen." Passive listening allows the speaker to develop his or her thoughts and ideas in the presence of another person who accepts but does not evaluate, who supports but does not intrude. By listening passively, you provide a supportive environment. Once that has been established, you may wish to participate in a more active way, verbally and nonverbally.

Fill in the blank above with the ONE most appropriate word from the passage. If necessary, change the word form. Then, complete the title of the second paragraph by filling in the blank below with the ONE most appropriate word from the passage. If necessary, change the word form.

The Definition And ____②____ of Passive Listening.

____

NOTE

Step 1	Survey
Key Words	
Signal Words	
Step 2	**Reading**
Purpose	
Pattern of Organization	
Tone	
Main Idea	
Step 3	**Summary**
지문 요약하기 (Paraphrasing)	
Step 4	**Recite**
요약문 말로 설명하기	

05 **Read the passage and follow the directions.** [2 points]

The costs associated with a traditional view of masculinity are enormous, and the damage occurs at both personal and societal levels. The belief that a boy should be tough(aggressive, competitive, and daring) can create emotional pain for him. While a few boys experience short-term success for their toughness, there is little security in the long run. Instead, it leads to a series of challenges which few, if any, boys ultimately win. There is no security in being at the top when so many other boys are competing for the same status. Toughness also leads to increased chances of stress, physical injury, and even early death. It is considered manly to take extreme physical risks and voluntarily engage in combative, hostile activities. The flip side of toughness—nurturance—is not a quality perceived as masculine and thus not valued. Because of this, boys and men experience a greater emotional distance from other people and few opportunities to participate in meaningful interpersonal relationships. Studies consistently show that fathers spend very small amounts of time interacting with their children. In addition, men report that they seldom have intimate relationships with other men. They are afraid of getting too close and don't know how to take down the walls that they have built between themselves.

What is the title for the passage? Write your answer by filling in the blank with below with the ONE most appropriate word from the passage.

The ________________ of Masculinity.

NOTE

Step 1	Survey
Key Words	
Signal Words	
Step 2	**Reading**
Purpose	
Pattern of Organization	
Tone	
Main Idea	
Step 3	**Summary**
지문 요약하기 (Paraphrasing)	
Step 4	**Recite**
요약문 말로 설명하기	

06 **Read the passage and follow the directions.** [2 points]

Wilbur and Orville Wright are usually credited with being the first to fly an airplane. On December 17, 1903, in Kitty Hawk, North Carolina, Orville flew the brothers' new invention for twelve seconds. However, some people argue that New Zealand farmer Richard Pearse, who designed his own engine-powered flying machine, was actually the first to fly when his craft rose fifty yards into the air on March 31, 1903, eight months before the Wrights' flight. Others argue that Gustave A. Whitehead deserves the credit for making the first powered flight. Although evidence such as eyewitness accounts is lacking, Whitehead supposedly flew his aircraft for the first time in Bridgeport, Connecticut, on August 14, 1901, more than two years before the Wrights' flight. Then there are those who insist that Brazilian Alberto Santos-Dumont was the first man to achieve powered flight when he flew his invention fifty meters on October 23, 1906. Because the Wrights launched their plane into the air with a catapult device and Santos-Dumont's plane, which had wheels, took off under its own power alone, his countrymen believe that he is actually the true Father of Aviation.

What is the title of the passage? Write your answer by filling in the blank below with FOUR consecutive words from the passage.

Different Points of View About the ______________________.

NOTE

Step 1	**Survey**
Key Words	
Signal Words	
Step 2	**Reading**
Purpose	
Pattern of Organization	
Tone	
Main Idea	
Step 3	**Summary**
지문 요약하기 (Paraphrasing)	
Step 4	**Recite**
요약문 말로 설명하기	

CHAPTER 03

빈칸추론

모범답안 및 번역 p.036

01 **Read the passage and follow the directions.** [2 points]

The celebrated philosopher William James proposed a distinction between voluntary and involuntary attention. When you cross a busy intersection, you are depleting finite reserves of voluntary, directed attention. The antidote is not to sit quietly in a darkened room. The environment has to have some kind of stimulation to activate your ______ⓐ______—your fascination. Urban environments can clearly elicit involuntary attention (honking horns in Times Square), but they do so in a harsh, peremptory way that requires voluntary attention to override. Natural environments, on the other hand, provide softly fascinating stimulation. Your eye is captured by the shape of a branch, a ripple in the water; your mind follows.

An eminent scholar conducted a study in which he sent volunteers on a fifty-minute walk through either an arboretum or city streets, then gave his subjects a cognitive assessment. Those who had taken the nature walk performed about twenty per cent better than their counterparts on tests of memory and attention. They also tended to be in a better mood, although that didn't affect their scores. However, people don't have to like the interaction with nature to get the benefits. Some of the walks took place in June, whereas others took place in January; most people didn't particularly enjoy trudging through the harsh Michigan winter, but their scores jumped just as much as in the summer trials. Not surprisingly, those whose directed ______ⓑ______ is most depleted seem to get the biggest benefits: an end-of-workday nature romp packs a greater restorative punch than one first thing in the morning, and the boost is five times bigger in people who have been diagnosed with clinical depression.

Fill in blank ⓐ with TWO words from the passage and fill in blank ⓑ with ONE word from the passage. If necessary, change the form of each word.

NOTE

Step 1	Survey
Key Words	
Signal Words	
Step 2	**Reading**
Purpose	
Pattern of Organization	
Tone	
Main Idea	
Step 3	**Summary**
지문 요약하기 (Paraphrasing)	
Step 4	**Recite**
요약문 말로 설명하기	

02 **Read the passage and follow the directions.** [2 points]

Sunlight is not the only forceful breeze that emanates from the Sun. There is another, known as the solar wind. The solar wind is a flood of plasma, protons and electrons, that streams out constantly from the Sun in all directions at a velocity of about 500 hm/s. We never encounter it here on Earth, because we are protected from it by the Earth's magnetosphere.

If the Earth's magnetosphere blocks the solar wind, it must be creating drag, and therefore feel a force as a result. Why not create an artificial magnetosphere on a spacecraft and use the same effect for propulsion? This was an idea that Boeing engineer Dana Andrews and I hit on in 1988. The idea was timely. In 1987, ______ⓐ______ had been discovered. These are essential to making a magnetic propulsion device practical, as low-temperature superconductors require too much heavy cooling equipment and ordinary conductors require too much power. The amount of force per square kilometer of solar wind is much less than that created by sunlight, but the area blocked off by a magnetic field could be made much larger than any practical solid solar sail. Working in collaboration, Dana and I derived equations and ran computer simulations of the solar wind impacting a spacecraft generating a large magnetic field.

Our results: If practical high-temperature superconducting cable can be made that can conduct electrical current with the same density as the state-of-the-art low-temperature superconductors such as niobium titanium, then magnetic sails or "magsails" can be made that will have thrust-to-weight ratios a hundred times better than that of a 10-micron-thick solar sail. Furthermore, unlike an ultra-thin solar sail, the ______ⓑ______ would not be difficult to deploy. Instead of being made of thin plastic film, it would be made of rugged cable, which due to magnetic forces would automatically "inflate" itself into a stiff hoop shape as soon as electrical current was put in it.

Fill in each blank with TWO words from the passage. If necessary, change the form of each word.

____

____

NOTE

Step 1	Survey
Key Words	
Signal Words	
Step 2	**Reading**
Purpose	
Pattern of Organization	
Tone	
Main Idea	
Step 3	**Summary**
지문 요약하기 (Paraphrasing)	
Step 4	**Recite**
요약문 말로 설명하기	

03 **Read the passage and follow the directions.** [2 points]

Fathers' rights as a civil liberties issue seems like a laughable bemoaning of one's patriarchal privilege. It appears anti-feminist: It's mostly men who run the world, no matter what Beyonce sings. But despite male dominance of government and business, disparities in pay and househould responsibility and even continued risk of sexual assault, real examples of male inequality should not be dismissed.

Unmarried men have little security in child rearing decisions and custody outcomes. Legally, the extent of decisions made by married men about reproduction and children stops at the sexual act. Beyond that, the mother has the most leverage to make decisions about visitation and possible adoption. Why? Because law and social practice assume that unmarried men in intimate relationships have no interest in commitment, stability or responsibility.

Of course, individuals and institutions have stories and numbers to "prove" that fathers should be treated differently than mothers because they're irresponsible. Old laws are illustrative of this assumption: Unmarried fathers would lose custody of their children upon the death of their mother, because the law deemed them inherently unfit, incapable and unstable. In a majority of states, adoptions can proceed even without the knowledge of the birth father, unless they can miraculously register as a putative father in advance of the birth.

But is it fair to characterize all unmarried men as deadbeats, just because they are not ____________? If men want fair treatment, this doesn't inherently mean they oppose women's equality or advancement. There are always going to be bad examples of fed up, angry, bitter men that spout invectives at feminists, their ex-wives and all women in general. But all papas are not rolling stones. There are just regular, earnest, nice guys that want simple due process rights as men and partners.

Fill in the blank with ONE word from the passage. If necessary, change the word form.

____

____

NOTE

Step 1	Survey
Key Words	
Signal Words	
Step 2	**Reading**
Purpose	
Pattern of Organization	
Tone	
Main Idea	
Step 3	**Summary**
지문 요약하기 (Paraphrasing)	
Step 4	**Recite**
요약문 말로 설명하기	

04 **Read the passage and follow the directions.** [2 points]

The diminution of individual liberty is likely to continue, since it has two continuing causes. On the one hand, modern technique makes society more organic; on the other hand, modern sociology makes men more and more aware of the causal laws in virtue of which one man's acts are useful or harmful to another man. If we are to justify any particular form of individual liberty in the scientific society of the future, we shall have to do it on the ground that that form of liberty is for the utility of society as a whole, but not in most cases on the ground that the acts concerned affect nobody but the agent.

Let us take some examples of traditional principles which appear no longer defensible. The first example that occurs to me is as regards the investment of capital. At present, within wide limits, any man who has money to invest may invest it as he chooses. This freedom was defended during the heyday of laissezfaire on the ground that the business which paid best was always the most socially useful. Few men nowadays would dare to maintain such a doctrine. Nevertheless the old freedom persists. It is clear that in a scientific society capital would be invested where its social ____________ is greatest, not where it earns the highest rate of profits. The rate of profits earned depends often upon quite accidental circumstances.

Fill in the blank with ONE word from the passage.

NOTE

Step 1	Survey
Key Words	
Signal Words	
Step 2	**Reading**
Purpose	
Pattern of Organization	
Tone	
Main Idea	
Step 3	**Summary**
지문 요약하기 (Paraphrasing)	
Step 4	**Recite**
요약문 말로 설명하기	

05 **Read the passage and fill in the blank below with ONE word from the passage.** [2 points]

Cannabis is a popular recreational drug and its legal status has been a source of enduring controversy. In a recent study, David Pagliaccio, Ph.D. and coauthors analyzed data from a group of twin/siblings to determine whether cannabis use was associated with brain volumes. To determine whether any significant differences could be attributed to predispositional /familial or causal factors, brain volumes were compared across twin/sibling pairs. Among 241 twin/sibling pairs, 89 pairs were discordant for cannabis exposure, 81 pairs were concordant for cannabis exposure and 71 pairs were concordantly unexposed to cannabis. Among all 482 study participants, cannabis exposure was related to smaller left amygdala and right ventral striatum volumes. Volume differences were in the range of normal variation.

However, brain volumes did not differ between siblings discordant for cannabis exposure. Both the exposed and unexposed siblings in pairs discordant for cannabis exposure showed smaller amygdala volumes relative to ____________ unexposed pairs. "When using a simple index of exposure (i.e. ever vs. never use), we found no evidence for the causal influence of cannabis exposure on amygdala volume. Future work characterizing the roles of causal and predispositional factors underpinning neural changes at various degrees of cannabis involvement may provide targets for substance abuse policy and prevention programs," the authors conclude.

____

____

NOTE

Step 1	Survey
Key Words	
Signal Words	
Step 2	**Reading**
Purpose	
Pattern of Organization	
Tone	
Main Idea	
Step 3	**Summary**
지문 요약하기 (Paraphrasing)	
Step 4	**Recite**
요약문 말로 설명하기	

06 **Read the passage and follow the directions.** [2 points]

In suggesting any curtailment of ______ⓐ______ there are always two quite distinct questions to be considered. The first is whether such a curtailment would be in the public interest if it were wisely carried out, and the second is whether it will be in the public interest when it is carried out with a certain measure of ignorance and perversity. These two questions are in theory quite distinct, but from the point of view of the government the second question does not exist, since every government believes itself entirely free from both ignorance and perversity. Every government, consequently, in so far as it is not restrained by traditional prejudices, will advocate more interference with liberty than is wise. When, therefore, we are considering what interferences with liberty might be theoretically justified, we must hesitate to draw the conclusion that they should be advocated in practice. I think it probable, however, that almost all interferences with liberty for which there is a(n) ______ⓑ______ justification will, in time, be carried out in practice, because scientific technique is gradually making governments so strong that they need not consider outside opinion. The result of this will be that governments will be able to interfere with individual liberty wherever in their opinion there is a sound reason for so doing, and for the reason just given, this will be much more often than it should be. For this reason scientific technique is likely to lead to a governmental tyranny which may in time prove disastrous.

Fill in each blank with the ONE most appropriate word from the passage respectively. If necessary, change the form of each word.

____

____

NOTE

Step 1	Survey
Key Words	
Signal Words	
Step 2	**Reading**
Purpose	
Pattern of Organization	
Tone	
Main Idea	
Step 3	**Summary**
지문 요약하기 (Paraphrasing)	
Step 4	**Recite**
요약문 말로 설명하기	

07 **Read the passage and follow the directions.** [2 points]

Pidgins and creoles are the outcome of the need of people not sharing a language to communicate but differ from national and international languages in that a pidgin does not begin as an already existing language or dialect selected to serve this purpose; it is rather a particular combination of two languages.

A pidgin is a marginal language which arises to fulfill certain restricted communication needs among people who have no common language. In the initial stages of contact the ______ⓐ______ is often limited to transactions where a detailed exchanged of ideas is not required and where a small vocabulary, drawn almost exclusively from one language, suffices. The syntactic structure of the pidgin is less complex and less flexible than the structures of the languages that were in contact, and though many pidgin features clearly reflect usages in the contact languages others are unique to the pidgin.

A creole arises when a pidgin becomes the mother tongue of a speech community. The simple structure that characterized the pidgin is carried over into the creole but since a creole, as a mother tongue, must be capable of expressing the whole range of human experience, the lexicon is expanded, and frequently a more elaborate syntactic system evolves. Since creoles are often not regarded as "real" languages and consequently considered as inferior, it is worth noting that, for example, both French and English may be the outcome of pidgins—in the first case through ______ⓑ______ between native Gauls and occupying Romans, and in the second through ______ⓑ______ between the native Anglo-Saxons and the Danes who settled on the east coast of England.

Fill in each blank ⓐ and ⓑ with ONE word from the passage respectively.

____

____

NOTE

Step 1	Survey
Key Words	
Signal Words	
Step 2	**Reading**
Purpose	
Pattern of Organization	
Tone	
Main Idea	
Step 3	**Summary**
지문 요약하기 (Paraphrasing)	
Step 4	**Recite**
요약문 말로 설명하기	

08 **Read the passage and follow the directions.** [2 points]

The neck of a giraffe isn't all that different from any other mammal's. There are seven neck vertebrae, like those of humans, but they are much bigger. How ____________ their long necks has long been the subject of debate, dating back to the early days of evolutionary theory. French naturalist Jean Baptiste Lamarck, for instance, suggested that the giraffe neck lengthened as the animals stretched to reach leaves high in trees, with a "nervous fluid" flowing into the neck to make it longer. The giraffe's offspring would inherit the longer neck, then stretch to reach even higher leaves, and that even longer neck would get passed on.

That's not how evolution works, though. Animals that had longer necks had some sort of advantage, and they were able to pass on their genes, eventually resulting in super-long necked animals. Just what that advantage might have been is still unknown. Perhaps the feature let giraffes access more food resources high in the treetops. But since female giraffes prefer males with longer necks, sexual selection might also be involved.

But what did that evolution look like? And when did it happen? Insight into those questions comes from a study done by Melinda Danowitz and colleagues, which analyzed neck vertebrae from 11 species—nine that are extinct, modern giraffes and okapi(Okapi look like a cross between a zebra and a deer, but they belong to the same family as giraffes).

Giraffes, it turns out, are not the first species in their lineage to have a long neck—they just have the longest one. The species started off with a shorter neck, 7.5 million years ago, when it first appeared on the scene, after which the neck became even longer. But the lengthening began even earlier in the giraffe's lineage, the fossil analysis revealed.

Fill in the blank above with TWO words from the passage. If necessary, change the form of the word.

NOTE

Step 1	Survey
Key Words	
Signal Words	
Step 2	**Reading**
Purpose	
Pattern of Organization	
Tone	
Main Idea	
Step 3	**Summary**
지문 요약하기 (Paraphrasing)	
Step 4	**Recite**
요약문 말로 설명하기	

09 **Read the passage and follow the directions.** [2 points]

Children learn new languages very easily, almost too easily. Most adults find foreign languages quite difficult. They must toil and struggle and put in long hours of hard work to make even small gains in their ability in a new language. But a child seems to just pick it up out of thin air. To a child, it is all play and no work. And to make it even more frustrating for the adult learner, the results of a child's language play are superior to the results of an adults' language struggle. It does not seem fair. One commonly held theory to explain this phenomenon is this: God has given young children a magical ability to learn new languages. This ability slowly disappears, and is completely gone by the time an adult begins the task of learning a new language. This theory is attractive for two reasons. First, it explains the phenomenon. Children learn a new language easily and adults do not because, according to the theory, the magic is limited to ______________. And second, this theory helps adult learners to accept their fate. With the magic gone, they find it a little easier to buckle down to their difficult studies, knowing that now there is no other way for them to learn a new language.

Fill in the blank with the ONE most appropriate word from the passage.

NOTE

Step 1	Survey
Key Words	
Signal Words	
Step 2	**Reading**
Purpose	
Pattern of Organization	
Tone	
Main Idea	
Step 3	**Summary**
지문 요약하기 (Paraphrasing)	
Step 4	**Recite**
요약문 말로 설명하기	

10 **Read the passage and follow the directions.** [2 points]

Electricity, like light, travels extremely fast, at 300,000 kilometers per second. It flows easily through metal wires. In particular, copper and silver are very good conductors of electricity. Electricity also generates heat as it flows through most objects. It can be controlled and utilized easily using many different technologies. Electricity is very useful because it can be converted into many kinds of ______①______. Electricity can be converted in to light using light bulbs, and even heat by using heating coils. It can also be converted into motion or even stored chemical energy. Electricity is used everywhere; to produce goods, provide services, and transport materials and people. Electricity also is used in commerce, agriculture, medicine, communications, entertainment, and a variety of other areas. Expanded uses for electricity are constantly being developed. Not only does electricity provide energy it also provides ______②______. A total of 510,595 workers were employed by electric utilities at the end of 1990 in a wide variety of jobs. From repairing power lines, to providing information to electricity customers, to constructing new power plants.

Fill in each blank with the ONE most appropriate word from the passage respectively.

NOTE

Step 1	Survey
Key Words	
Signal Words	
Step 2	**Reading**
Purpose	
Pattern of Organization	
Tone	
Main Idea	
Step 3	**Summary**
지문 요약하기 (Paraphrasing)	
Step 4	**Recite**
요약문 말로 설명하기	

11 **Read the passage and follow the directions.** [2 points]

One of the things is you have to be able to find a really interesting problem that is soluble, that you don't have to wait for exploration to Jupiter to solve, and yet is an important problem. They're not in Antarctica or on Mars. They're right around us in the air. I heard a wonderful talk in this very building about black holes. There may be billions of microscopic black holes in every room in Dwinelle. It was a brilliant talk. You can see that what we don't know is right around us. Somebody once said if the fish were going to study the world, the last thing they would discover would be the ocean. Because we're so immersed in everyday things. A scientist is very different than a scientific worker. Most of the people that society calls "scientists" are what I call "scientific workers." A scientist is very much like a ____________. You do your best work lying awake in the afternoon. You have dreams and you have random thoughts and you have motivations that you don't understand, and stray bits of information that you put together from different sources, and you get an idea. And this idea is like a poem. John Keats, who was a doctor as well as a poet, just would suddenly—some beautiful lines of poetry would come into his head. I think that's the way real scientists work.

Fill in the blank with ONE word from the passage.

____

____

NOTE

Step 1	Survey
Key Words	
Signal Words	
Step 2	**Reading**
Purpose	
Pattern of Organization	
Tone	
Main Idea	
Step 3	**Summary**
지문 요약하기 (Paraphrasing)	
Step 4	**Recite**
요약문 말로 설명하기	

12 **Read the passage and follow the directions.** [2 points]

The early twentieth century marked a period of rapid industrial and technological change in a society which began to redefine the roles of the ______①______ and society. Max Weber and Sigmund Freud were two revolutionary thinkers of the time who recognized the importance of this relationship and tried to determine whether the power balance between society and the individual was tilted in one particular direction or the other. A world becoming an increasingly complex and restrictive forced these thinkers to ask themselves if society had indeed finally become a force too dynamic for the individual to manipulate; that if in fact it was society that had mastered the man. Although both thinkers provide radically different views of culture and society they are both essentially trying to answer the same question: does the individual control society or does society control the individual?

The relevance of such an argument might first be debated, for one might first respond to this question with some doubt; surely we have control of ourselves, do we all not have control of our own faculties at this very moment? At this moment you are reading or being subjected to a reading of this paper, therefore if this indeed is not fulfilling some immediate obvious desire it is accomplishing some sort of other goal. Likely this goal is to achieve an education but again we might ask ourselves why? Surely we all want to further our scholarly qualities and develop our minds but more likely this again has an underlying goal: to ______②______ in society. Society has shown us that in most cases it requires a good deal of education in order to succeed. Therefore we might entertain the question, is our presence here a product of our own desires or that of society's? The point of this reasoning is only to point out something we may not immediately recognize: regardless of what our own free will may dictate, we cannot help but be influenced by the values and morals of modern-day society.

Fill in each blank with ONE word from the passage.

NOTE

Step 1	Survey
Key Words	
Signal Words	
Step 2	**Reading**
Purpose	
Pattern of Organization	
Tone	
Main Idea	
Step 3	**Summary**
지문 요약하기 (Paraphrasing)	
Step 4	**Recite**
요약문 말로 설명하기	

13 **Read the passage and follow the directions.** [2 points]

Fatigue is of many sorts, some of which are a much graver obstacle to happiness than others. Purely ____ⓐ____, provided it is not excessive, tends if anything to be a cause of happiness; it leads to sound sleep and a good appetite, and gives zest to the pleasures that are possible on holidays. But when it is excessive it becomes a very grave evil. Peasant women in all but the most advanced communities are old at thirty, worn out with excessive toil. Children in the early days of industrialism were stunted in their growth and frequently killed by overwork in early years. The same thing still happens in China and Japan, where industrialism is new; to some extent also in the Southern States of America. Physical labour carried beyond a certain point is atrocious torture, and it has very frequently been carried so far as to make life all but unbearable. In the most advanced parts of the modern world, however, physical fatigue has been much minimized through the improvement of industrial conditions. The kind of fatigue that is most serious in the present day in advanced communities is ____ⓑ____. This kind, oddly enough, is most pronounced among the well-to-do, and tends to be much less among wage-earners than it is among business men and brain-workers. To escape from nervous fatigue in modern life is a very difficult thing.

Fill in each blank with the TWO most appropriate words from the passage.

NOTE

Step 1	Survey
Key Words	
Signal Words	
Step 2	**Reading**
Purpose	
Pattern of Organization	
Tone	
Main Idea	
Step 3	**Summary**
지문 요약하기 (Paraphrasing)	
Step 4	**Recite**
요약문 말로 설명하기	

14 **Read the passage and follow the directions.** [2 points]

> The race to the bottom is a socioeconomic concept that occurs between nations. When competition becomes fierce between nations over a particular area of trade and production, the nations are given increased incentive to dismantle currently existing regulatory standards. It may be seen that with the global push towards free trade, labor is now very susceptible to the race to the bottom model. With an extremely large labor pool to draw from worldwide and a virtually unrestricted ability to move capital, multi-national corporations may now freely move their operations from country to country, following the most affordable labor. This in turn affects labor laws, particularly in developing countries, where things such as minimum wage or required overtime pay create a large barrier to lowest-cost labor. The ____________, therefore, dictates that more and more nations (again, particularly in the developing world) will eliminate their labor laws.

Fill in the blank with the most appropriate words from the passage.

NOTE

Step 1	Survey
Key Words	
Signal Words	
Step 2	**Reading**
Purpose	
Pattern of Organization	
Tone	
Main Idea	
Step 3	**Summary**
지문 요약하기 (Paraphrasing)	
Step 4	**Recite**
요약문 말로 설명하기	

15 **Read the passage and follow the directions.** [2 points]

When we know the initial conditions of an orderly system, we can make ____①____ about it. For example, in the Newtonian macroworld, knowing with precision the initial conditions lets us state where a planet will be after a certain time, where a launched rocket will land, and when an eclipse will occur. Similarly, in the quantum microworld we can predict where an electron is likely to be in an atom, and the probability that a radioactive particle will decay in a given time interval. Predictability in orderly systems, both Newtonian and quantum, depends on knowledge of initial conditions. Some systems, however, whether Newtonian or quantum, are not orderly—they are inherently unpredictable. These are called "chaotic systems." Turbulent water flow is an example. No matter how precisely we know the initial conditions of a piece of floating wood as it flows downstream, we cannot predict its location later downstream. A feature of chaotic systems is that slight differences in initial conditions result in wildly different outcomes later. Two identical pieces of wood just slightly apart at one time are vastly far apart soon thereafter. Weather is ____②____. Small changes in one day's weather can produce big (and largely unpredictable) changes a week later. Meteorologists try their best, but they are bucking the hard fact of chaos in nature. This barrier to good prediction first led the scientist Edward Lorenz to ask, "Does the flap of a butterfly's wings in Brazil set off a tornado in Texas?" Now we talk about the "butterfly effect" when we are dealing with situations where very small effects can amplify into very big effects.

Fill in each blank with ONE word from the passage. If necessary, change each word form.

____

____

NOTE

Step 1	Survey
Key Words	
Signal Words	
Step 2	**Reading**
Purpose	
Pattern of Organization	
Tone	
Main Idea	
Step 3	**Summary**
지문 요약하기 (Paraphrasing)	
Step 4	**Recite**
요약문 말로 설명하기	

16 **Read the passage and follow the directions.** [2 points]

Observation depends on ______①______ and knowledge. If three friends travel abroad, one an architect, another a botanist, and the third a stockbroker, then the architect is likely to notice the style of houses and other buildings more than his friends do, because he is specially interested in them. The botanist will observe especially the flowers and trees of the country more than his friends; and s/he will actually see more details because s/he knows what to look for. Observation is guided by knowledge and prompted by interest. We have, however, no reason to suppose that the botanist, trained in such observation, or the architect, keenly observant of the buildings, will be more observant than the stockbroker of the faces of the foreign people they meet, or the dress of the women. Indeed, they are more likely to have their attention diverted by the objects of their special interests. So training in the careful ______②______ of the varied endings of Latin words, or of the changes in chemical substances in experiments, will have no effect on the observation of pictures or the movement of stars.

Fill in each blank with the ONE most appropriate word from the passage.

NOTE

Step 1	Survey
Key Words	
Signal Words	
Step 2	**Reading**
Purpose	
Pattern of Organization	
Tone	
Main Idea	
Step 3	**Summary**
지문 요약하기 (Paraphrasing)	
Step 4	**Recite**
요약문 말로 설명하기	

17 **Read the passage and follow the directions.** [2 points]

The concept of sustainability applies to all aspects of life on Earth and is commonly defined within ______①______, social and economic contexts. Due to factors such as overpopulation, lack of education, inadequate financial circumstances and the actions of past generations, sustainability can be difficult to achieve. In an ecological context, sustainability is defined as the ability of an ecosystem to maintain ecological processes, functions, biodiversity and productivity into the future. In a social context, sustainability is expressed as meeting the needs of the present without compromising the ability of future generations to meet their own needs. When applied in an economic context, a business is sustainable if it has adapted its practices for the use of renewable resources and is accountable for the environmental impacts of its activities. To be sustainable, regardless of context, Earth's resources must be used at a rate at which they can be replenished. There is now clear scientific evidence that humanity is living unsustainably, and that an effort is needed to keep human use of Earth's resources within ______②______ limits.

Fill in each blank with the ONE most appropriate word from the passage.

NOTE

Step 1	Survey
Key Words	
Signal Words	
Step 2	**Reading**
Purpose	
Pattern of Organization	
Tone	
Main Idea	
Step 3	**Summary**
지문 요약하기 (Paraphrasing)	
Step 4	**Recite**
요약문 말로 설명하기	

18 **Read the passage and follow the directions.** [2 points]

In the early factories the employers went so far as to manipulate their clocks or sound their factory whistles at the wrong times in order to cheat the workers out of a little of this valuable new commodity. Later such practices became less frequent, but the influence of the clock imposed regularity on the lives of the majority of men that had previously been known only in the monasteries. Men actually became like clocks, acting with a repetitive _____①_____ which had no resemblance to the rhythmic life of a natural being. They became, as the Victorian phrase put it, "as regular as clockwork." Only in the country districts where the natural lives of animals and plants and the elements still dominated existence, did any large proportion of the population fail to yield to the deadly tick of monotony.

At first this new attitude to time, this new regularity of life, was imposed by the clock-owning masters on the unwilling poor. The factory slave reacted in his spare time by living with a chaotic irregularity which characterized the slums of early nineteenth-century industrialism. Men fled to the timeless worlds of drink or Methodist inspiration. But gradually the idea of regularity spread downwards and among the workers. Nineteenth-century religion and morality played their part by proclaiming the sin of "wasting time." The introduction of mass-produced watches and clocks in the 1850s spread time-consciousness among those who had previously merely reacted to the stimulus of the knocker-up or the factory whistle. In the church and the school, in the office and the workshop, _____②_____ was held up as the greatest of the virtues.

Fill in the blanks ① and ② respectively with the ONE most appropriate word from the passage.

NOTE

Step 1	Survey
Key Words	
Signal Words	
Step 2	**Reading**
Purpose	
Pattern of Organization	
Tone	
Main Idea	
Step 3	**Summary**
지문 요약하기 (Paraphrasing)	
Step 4	**Recite**
요약문 말로 설명하기	

19 **Read the passage and follow the directions.** [2 points]

Standardized entrance exams have played a major role in the college-admissions process since the late 1920s, and their significance has grown over the past several decades. The prominence of these tests, however, has been coupled with controversy about their ____①____ and effectiveness in determining college success. College entrance exams, in particular the SAT, have been targets of criticism for years. Critics claim that the exams are biased against minorities, women and low-income students; lack fairness in how they sort students; and contribute to an overly competitive admissions process. Futhermore, students are under pressure to increase their scores for admissions and financial aid purposes; teachers are under pressure to help students score well; and colleges and universities are under pressure to admit students with high scores to improve their rankings and fundraising abilities. Detractors have long argued that far too much emphasis is placed on ____②____ for college admissions that, in their opinion, do not accurately reflect the range of student talents or their commitment to succeed at the postsecondary level.

Fill in each blank with the ONE or TWO most appropriate word(s) from the passage respectively. If necessary, change each word form.

___

___

NOTE

Step 1	Survey
Key Words	
Signal Words	
Step 2	**Reading**
Purpose	
Pattern of Organization	
Tone	
Main Idea	
Step 3	**Summary**
지문 요약하기 (Paraphrasing)	
Step 4	**Recite**
요약문 말로 설명하기	

20 **Read the passage and follow the directions.** [2 points]

> Throughout human history, men have been generally engaged in social life such as laboring for money and food and public gathering for power; hence, men have looked for ______①______. On the other hand, it has been women who acquired their happiness by bearing and rearing children. In women's view, public accomplishment makes a man attractive and desirable as a marriage partner or a father of future children. But for men, the condition is the opposite. The more a woman tries to accomplish socially, the less charming and desirable she seems to a man as a wife. This gender bias, however, does not appear to be quite evidenced, especially in the modern societies in terms of economic and technical development, due to the fact that more women prefer to have jobs than to raise children and that more ______②______ seem to be settled in the house to run household affairs.

Fill in blank ① with the TWO most appropriate consecutive words from the passage. Then fill in blank ② with ONE word from the passage.

____

____

NOTE

Step 1	Survey
Key Words	
Signal Words	
Step 2	**Reading**
Purpose	
Pattern of Organization	
Tone	
Main Idea	
Step 3	**Summary**
지문 요약하기 (Paraphrasing)	
Step 4	**Recite**
요약문 말로 설명하기	

21 **Read the passage and follow the directions.** [2 points]

In medieval times rivers were the veins of the body politic as well as economic. Boundaries between states or shires, they were crossed by fords which became the sites of towns, or by bridges which were often points of battle. Upon rivers the people of that time depended for food, ______①______ and transport. In our day fish are caught in the sea and brought to us by rail and lorry; only the angler still thinks fresh-water fish important, and pollution of rivers drives him into smaller and smaller reaches in which to practice his sport. But in earlier times, when sea fish were eaten only by those who lived on the sea coast, when meat was obtainable only for part of the year, and when fasts were frequent and universally practiced, river fish played an important part in the national life. Every abbey and great man's house had its fish pond, and across the rivers great and small stretched the fish weirs, usually made of stakes and nets or basketwork. Between the owners of the fisheries and the bargemaster who needed an unimpeded passage continuous war was fought, till the importance of freshwater fish lessened as the practice of fasting ceased to be universal, as meat became available all the year round, and as the transport of ______②______ inland became practicable. Rivers were also the most important source of power. Every stream had its mills, not only for grinding corn, but for all the other industrial processes of the time, such as fulling cloth or driving the hammers of ironworks. Placed down the bank wherever a head of water could be got, these mills were to be found on the tiny stream that ran through a village, or on the bigger river that was also used for navigation.

Fill in blank ① with the ONE most appropriate word from the passage. Then fill in the second blank with TWO words from the passage.

____

____

NOTE

Step 1	Survey
Key Words	
Signal Words	
Step 2	**Reading**
Purpose	
Pattern of Organization	
Tone	
Main Idea	
Step 3	**Summary**
지문 요약하기 (Paraphrasing)	
Step 4	**Recite**
요약문 말로 설명하기	

04 지칭추론

모범답안 및 번역 p.078

01 **Read the passage and follow the directions.** [2 points]

A new study shows that broad developmental changes occur when honey bee larvae—those destined to be workers—are switched from eating royal jelly to a diet of jelly that includes honey and beebread(a type of processed pollen).

Beebread and honey contain p-coumaric acid, but royal jelly does not. Queens feed exclusively on royal jelly. Worker bees known as nurses feed the larvae according to the needs of the hive. Experiments revealed that ingesting p-coumaric acid pushes the honey bee larvae down a different developmental pathway from those fed only royal jelly. Some genes, about a third of the honey bee genome, are upregulated and another third are downregulated, changing the landscape of proteins available to help fight disease or develop the bees' reproductive parts.

Consuming the phytochemical p-coumaric acid, which is ubiquitous in beebread and honey, alters the expression of a whole suite of genes involved in caste determination. For years, people have wondered what components in royal jelly lead to queen development, but what might be more important is what isn't in royal jelly—plant chemicals that can interfere with development.

While previous molecular studies have provided simple snapshots of the gene transcript variations that are associated with the exposure of insects to natural and synthetic chemicals, the genomics approaches used in this study offer a significantly more complex perspective on the biochemical and physiological processes occurring in plant-insect interactions.

What is the new discovery on honey bee colonies? Write your answer by filling in the blank with TWO consecutive words from the passage.

A study on how honey bee colonies determine which larvae will serve as workers and which will become queens reveals that ____________ play(s) a key role in the bees' developmental fate.

NOTE

Step 1	Survey
Key Words	
Signal Words	
Step 2	**Reading**
Purpose	
Pattern of Organization	
Tone	
Main Idea	
Step 3	**Summary**
지문 요약하기 (Paraphrasing)	
Step 4	**Recite**
요약문 말로 설명하기	

02 **Read the passage and follow the directions.** [2 points]

There are many <u>sources of false belief</u> besides self-importance. One of these is love of the marvelous. I knew at one time a scientifically-minded conjuror, who used to perform his tricks before a small audience, and then get them, each separately, to write down what they had seen happen. Almost always they wrote down something much more astonishing than the reality, and usually something which no conjuror could have achieved; yet they all thought they were reporting truly what they had seen with their own eyes. This sort of falsification is still more true of rumors. A tells B that last night he saw Mr.-, the eminent prohibitionist, slightly the worse for liquor; B tells C that A saw the good man reeling drunk, C tells D that he was picked up unconscious in the ditch, D tells E that he is well known to pass out every evening. Here, it is true, another motive comes in, namely malice. We like to think ill of our neighbors, and are prepared to believe the worst on very little evidence. But even where there is no such motive, what is marvelous is readily believed unless it goes against some strong prejudice. All history until the eighteenth century is full of prodigies and wonders which modern historians ignore, not because they are less well attested than facts which the historians accept, but because modern taste among the learned prefers what science regards as probable.

According to the writer of the passage, what are the "sources of false belief"? Write your answer by filling in blank ⓐ and ⓑ with the word(s) from the passage.

The three sources of false belief are _____ⓐ_____, _____ⓑ_____ and malice.

NOTE

Step 1	Survey
Key Words	
Signal Words	
Step 2	**Reading**
Purpose	
Pattern of Organization	
Tone	
Main Idea	
Step 3	**Summary**
지문 요약하기 (Paraphrasing)	
Step 4	**Recite**
요약문 말로 설명하기	

03 **Read the passage and follow the directions.** [2 points]

> For women, as for girls, intimacy is the fabric of relationships, and talk is the thread from which it is woven. Little girls create and maintain friendships by exchanging secrets; similarly, women regard conversation as the cornerstone of friendship. So a woman expects her husband to be a new and improved version of a best friend. What is important is not the individual subjects that are discussed but the sense of closeness, of a life shared, that emerges when people tell their thoughts, feelings, and impressions. Bonds between boys can be as intense as girls', but they are based less on talking, more on doing things together. Since they don't assume talk is the cement that binds a relationship, men don't know what kind of talk women want, and they don't miss ⓐ it when it isn't there. Boys' groups are larger, more inclusive, and more hierarchical, so boys must struggle to avoid the subordinate position in the group. This may play a role in women's complaints that men don't listen to them. Some men really don't like to listen, because being the listener makes them feel one-down, like a child listening to adults or an employee to a boss.

Identify to what the underlined "it" refers.

___

___

NOTE

Step 1	Survey
Key Words	
Signal Words	
Step 2	**Reading**
Purpose	
Pattern of Organization	
Tone	
Main Idea	
Step 3	**Summary**
지문 요약하기 (Paraphrasing)	
Step 4	**Recite**
요약문 말로 설명하기	

04 **Read the passage and follow the directions.** [4 points]

There is lots of zip in DNA-based biology today. With each passing year it incorporates an ever increasing fraction of the life sciences, ranging from single-cell organisms, like bacteria and yeast, to the complexities of the human brain. All this wonderful frenzy was unimaginable when I first entered the world of genetics. In 1948, biology was an all too descriptive discipline near the bottom of science's totem pole, with physics at its top. By then Einstein's turn-of-the century ideas about the interconversion of matter and energy had been transformed into the powers of atom. If not held in check, the nuclear weapons they made possible might well destroy the very fabric of civilized human life. So physicists of the late 1940s were simultaneously revered for making atoms relevant to society and feared for what ① <u>their toys</u> could do if they were to fall into the hands of evil. Such ambivalent feelings are now widely held toward ____②____. The double-helical structure of DNA, initially admired for its intellectual simplicity, today represents to many a double-edged sword that can be used for evil as well as good.

Identify from the passage what the underlined "their toys" refer to. Second, fill in the blank with the ONE word from the passage.

NOTE

Step 1	Survey
Key Words	
Signal Words	
Step 2	**Reading**
Purpose	
Pattern of Organization	
Tone	
Main Idea	
Step 3	**Summary**
지문 요약하기 (Paraphrasing)	
Step 4	**Recite**
요약문 말로 설명하기	

05 **Read the passage and follow the directions.** [2 points]

For years, critics have argued about the ancient Greek play *Oedipus Rex*. Some have claimed that Oedipus knows nothing of his guilt until the end of the play, when it is revealed that he murdered his own father. Others have insisted that Oedipus is aware all along of his guilt. According to this point of view, Oedipus, the brilliant solver of riddles, could not possibly have ignored the mounting evidence that he was the king's murderer. Just how or why this debate has raged for so many years remains a mystery. The correct interpretations are so obvious. Oedipus knows from the beginning that he is guilty. He just pretends to be ignorant of the truth. For example, when a servant tells the story of the king's murder, he uses the word "bandits." But when Oedipus repeats this story, he uses the singular form "bandit." Sophocles provides clues like this throughout the play. Thus, it's hard to understand why anyone would think that Oedipus does not know the truth.

Describe to what the underlined "the truth" refers.

NOTE

Step 1	Survey
Key Words	
Signal Words	
Step 2	**Reading**
Purpose	
Pattern of Organization	
Tone	
Main Idea	
Step 3	**Summary**
지문 요약하기 (Paraphrasing)	
Step 4	**Recite**
요약문 말로 설명하기	

06 **Read the passage and follow the directions.** [2 points]

Pain has plagued us throughout the history of our species. We spend our lives trying to avoid it, and, from one point of view, what we call "happiness" may be just the absence of pain. Yet it is difficult to define pain, which may be sharp, dull, shooting, throbbing, imaginary, or referred. We have many pains that surge from within as cramps and aches. And we also talk about emotional distress as pain. Pains are often combined, the emotional with the physical, and the physical with the physical. When you burn yourself, the skin swells and blisters, and when the blister breaks, the skin hurts in yet another way. A wound may become infected. Then histamine and serotonin are released, which dilate the blood vessels and trigger a pain response. Not all internal injuries can be felt (it's possible to do brain surgery under a local anesthetic), but illnesses that constrict blood flow often are: Angina pectoris, for example, which occurs when the coronary arteries shrink too tight for blood to comfortably pass. Even intense pain often eludes accurate description, as Virginia Woolf reminds us in her essay "On Being Ill": "<u>English, which can express the thoughts of Hamlet and the tragedy of Lear, has few words for the shiver and the headache ... let a sufferer try to describe a pain in his head to a doctor and language at once runs dry</u>."

What does the underlined part mean? Write your answer by filling in each blank with ONE word from the passage. The first word should be capitalized.

____ⓐ____ is almost impossible to put into ____ⓑ____.

NOTE

Step 1	Survey
Key Words	
Signal Words	
Step 2	**Reading**
Purpose	
Pattern of Organization	
Tone	
Main Idea	
Step 3	**Summary**
지문 요약하기 (Paraphrasing)	
Step 4	**Recite**
요약문 말로 설명하기	

07 **Read the passage and follow the directions.** [2 points]

People are always talking about 'the problem of youth'. If there is one—which I take leave to doubt—then, it is older people who create it, not the young themselves. Let us get down to fundamentals and agree that the young are after all human beings—people just like their elders. There is only one difference between an old man and a young one: the young man has a glorious future before him and the old one has a splendid future behind him: and maybe that is where the rub is. When I was a teenager, I felt that I was just young and uncertain—that I was a new boy in a huge school, and I would have been very pleased to be regarded as something so interesting as a problem. For one thing, being a problem gives you a certain identity, and that is one of the things the young are busily engaged in seeking. I find young people exciting. They have an air of freedom, and they have not a dreary commitment to mean ambitions or ① <u>love of comfort</u>. They are not anxious ② <u>social climbers</u>, and they have no devotion to ③ <u>material things</u>. All this seems to me to link them with life, and the ④ <u>origins of things</u>. It's as if they were in some sense cosmic beings in violent and lovely contrast with us ⑤ <u>suburban creatures</u>. All that is in my mind when I meet a young person. He may be conceited, illmannered, presumptuous or fatuous, but I do not turn for protection to dreary clichés about respect for elders—as if mere age were a reason for respect. I accept that we are equals, and I will argue with him, as an equal, if I think he is wrong.

Which one among ①~⑤ is different from the rest in terms of the meaning of reference? Write the number.

NOTE

Step 1	Survey
Key Words	
Signal Words	
Step 2	**Reading**
Purpose	
Pattern of Organization	
Tone	
Main Idea	
Step 3	**Summary**
지문 요약하기 (Paraphrasing)	
Step 4	**Recite**
요약문 말로 설명하기	

08 **Read the passage and follow the directions.** [2 points]

"To have" is a deceptively simple expression. Every human being has something: a body, clothes, shelter—on up to the modern man or woman who has a car, a television set, a washing machine, etc. Living without having something is virtually impossible. Why then should having be a problem? Yet the linguistic history of "having" indicates that the word is indeed a problem. To those who believe that to have is a most natural category of human existence, it may come as a surprise to learn that many languages have no word for "to have." In Hebrew, for instance, "I have" must be expressed by the indirect form *jesh li* ("there is to me"). In fact, languages that express possession in this way rather than by "I have," predominate. It is interesting to note that in the development of many languages, the construction "there is to me" is followed later on by the construction "I have," but as Emile Benveniste has pointed out, the evolution does not occur <u>in the reverse direction</u>. This fact suggests that the word for "to have" develops in connection with the development of private property, while it is absent in societies with predominantly functional property, that is, possession for use.

Identify to what the underlined "the reverse direction" refer.

____

____

NOTE

Step 1	Survey
Key Words	
Signal Words	
Step 2	**Reading**
Purpose	
Pattern of Organization	
Tone	
Main Idea	
Step 3	**Summary**
지문 요약하기 (Paraphrasing)	
Step 4	**Recite**
요약문 말로 설명하기	

09 **Read the passage and follow the directions.** [2 points]

Modern European and American history is centered around the effort to gain freedom from the political, economic, and spiritual shackles that have bound men. The battles for freedom were fought by the oppressed, those who wanted new liberties, against those who had privileges to defend. While a class was fighting for its own liberation from domination, it believed itself to be fighting for human freedom as such and thus was able to appeal to an ideal, to the longing for freedom rooted in all who are oppressed. Despite many reversals, freedom has won battles. Many died in those battles in the conviction that to die in the struggle against oppression was better than to live without freedom. Such a death was the utmost assertion of their individuality. History seemed to be proving that it was possible for man to govern himself, to make decisions for himself, and to think and feel as he saw fit. The full expression of man's potentialities seemed to be the goal towards which social development was rapidly approaching. The principles of economic liberalism, political democracy, religious autonomy, and individualism in personal life, gave expression to the longing for freedom, and at the same time seemed to bring mankind nearer to its realization. One tie after another was severed. Man had overthrown the domination of nature and made himself her master; he had overthrown the domination of the Church and the domination of the absolutist state. The abolition of external domination seemed to be not only a necessary but also a sufficient condition to attain the cherished goal: freedom of the individual.

Identify to what the underlined phrase "One tie after another" refers.

___

___

NOTE

Step 1	Survey
Key Words	
Signal Words	
Step 2	**Reading**
Purpose	
Pattern of Organization	
Tone	
Main Idea	
Step 3	**Summary**
지문 요약하기 (Paraphrasing)	
Step 4	**Recite**
요약문 말로 설명하기	

유희태 일반영어 ②

2S2R

유형

_Part

02

서술형

CHAPTER

01 의미찾기

모범답안 및 번역 p.098

01 **Read the passage and follow the directions.** [4 points]

The newspaper must provide for the reader the facts, unslanted, objectively selected facts. But in these days of complex news it must provide more; it must supply interpretation, the meaning of the facts. This is the most important assignment confronting American journalism—to make clear to the reader the problems of the day, to make international news as understandable as community news, to recognize that there is no longer any such thing as "local" news, because any event in the international area has a local reaction in manpower draft, in economic strain, in terms, indeed, of our very way of life. There is in journalism a widespread view that when you embark on interpretation, you are entering choppy and dangerous waters, the swirling tides of opinion. This is nonsense.

The opponents of interpretation insist that the writer and the editor shall confine themselves to the "facts." This insistence raises two questions. As to the first query, consider how a so-called "factual" story comes about. The reporter collects, say, fifty facts; out of these fifty, his space allotment being necessarily restricted, he selects the ten, which he considers most important. This is Judgment Number One. Then he or his editor decides which of these ten facts shall constitute the lead of the piece. This is important decision because many readers do not proceed beyond the first paragraph. This is Judgment Number Two. Then the night editor determines whether the article shall be presented on page one, where it has a large impact, or on page twenty-four, where it has little. Judgment Number Three.

Thus, in the presentation of a so-called "factual" or "objective" story, at least three judgments are involved. And they are judgments not at all unlike those involved in ____________, in which reporter and editor, calling upon their general background, and their "news neutralism", arrive at a conclusion as to the significance of the news. The two areas of judgment, presentation of the news and its interpretation, are both objective rather than subjective processes—as objective, that is, as any human being can be. If an editor is intent on slanting the news, he can do it in other ways and more effectively than by interpretation. He can do it by the selection of those facts that prop up his particular plea. Or he can do it by the play he gives a story—promoting it to page one or demoting it to page thirty.

Describe what "Judgment Number One" and what "Judgment Number Three" are. Also, in what way are presentation and interpretation of news similar? While making your answer, do not copy more than FOUR consecutive words from the passage. Third, fill in the blank with the ONE most appropriate word from the passage.

____

____

____

____

____

NOTE

Step 1	Survey
Key Words	
Signal Words	
Step 2	**Reading**
Purpose	
Pattern of Organization	
Tone	
Main Idea	
Step 3	**Summary**
지문 요약하기 (Paraphrasing)	
Step 4	**Recite**
요약문 말로 설명하기	

MEMO

02 **Read the passage and follow the directions.** [4 points]

Personal independence is such an iconic American value today that few of us question it. In previous generations, retirees lived with family, but now that a large swath of older people can afford to live on their own, that's what they choose. The convenience of digital devices means that we can now work, shop and pay our bills online, without dealing directly with other people. 10% of Americans work alone in remote offices and over 13% live alone, the highest rate of solo living in American history.

Many researches, however, suggest that, even if you enjoy being by yourself, it just might kill you—or at least shorten your life. Living alone, or simply spending a lot of your time on your own, can compromise your physical and psychological resilience—whether or not you like your solitude. If you fit into one of following categories—living alone, spending much of your time alone or often feeling solitary—your risk of dying within the next seven years is about 30% higher than it is for people who are otherwise like you. In-person interaction has physiological effects.

① A landmark longitudinal study published in the American Journal of Epidemiology in 1979 followed nearly every resident of a northern California town for nine years; its results showed that people who not only had intimate partners but met regularly with others to play bridge or volunteer at church were twice as likely to outlive those who led ____②____ lives. Still, critics wondered whether social contact was the key. Perhaps the social butterflies were healthier to begin with, or the more isolated people had hidden problems, such as depression or disability, that cut their lives short. A team led by Dr. Julianne Holt controlled for these confounding factors. What's more, they discovered that the effect isn't always a matter of preference or state of mind. We used to think that subjective experience was all that mattered. You could be single or married, spend your days alone or in a throng of people; if you often felt lonely, the thinking went, your blood pressure would spike and your immune function would suffer.

The new research found, however, that objective measures of the amount of human contact you get are as critical to your survival as your opinion of your social life. "I've spent almost my whole career studying social support, and I absolutely know the strong effects that our perceptions have on our physiology," Dr. Holt said. "But there are other determinants of health that are independent of our perceptions.

Describe what the "landmark longitudinal study" discovered regarding lifespan. Also, how is the study led by Dr. Holt is different from the landmark study? When you answer these questions, do not copy more than FIVE consecutive words from the passage. Third, fill in the blank with ONE most appropriate word from the passage.

NOTE

Step 1	Survey
Key Words	
Signal Words	
Step 2	**Reading**
Purpose	
Pattern of Organization	
Tone	
Main Idea	
Step 3	**Summary**
지문 요약하기 (Paraphrasing)	
Step 4	**Recite**
요약문 말로 설명하기	

MEMO

03 **Read the passage and follow the directions.** [4 points]

Whether they trust it or not, consumers aren't exactly avoiding G.M. foods, at least in some places. It's hard to find a soybean or a kernel of corn in North America that's not genetically modified. That G.M. foods are so prevalent in the region may not be realized because American food providers are not required to disclose G.M.O. content. There seems to be little clamor for such information, either; in a 2012 referendum in health-conscious California, voters narrowly declined to require labeling. Labeling rules are stricter in Europe, and far less G.M. food is produced or consumed there. A European Commission decision in April allowing member states to restrict the use of G.M.O.s approved at the regional level suggests that the public isn't warming to them.

G.M. crops are becoming more prevalent in the developing world, however. Their use is permitted across Latin America, Asia and Africa. Brazil is the second-largest producer, after the United States, followed by Argentina. Extensive cultivation of G.M.O.s also occurs in China, Paraguay and South Africa. In 2012, for the first time, the area planted with G.M. crops in developing countries was higher than in developed countries. Their grip hasn't loosened since then. Farmers in the developing world planted about 95 million hectares (235 million acres) of G.M. crops in 2014, five times more than in 2003. That compares with a doubling in industrial countries, to about 86 million hectares. One reason for the appeal in emerging economies is clear. Increases in yields and profits with G.M. crops were substantially greater there than in mature economies. The developing world is also where a lot of hunger exists, and much hope is being pinned on the success of G.M. crops to alleviate it.

But as with other aspects of G.M.O.s, doubts have been raised about their utility in reducing hunger and increasing the global food supply. Some researchers contend that indoor farming can do both in a more benign way. Having total control over light, water and other factors allows food to grow much faster than outdoors, they say. The United Nations World Food Program makes the case that limited supply isn't the primary reason for food shortages. Lack of investment in infrastructure that gets food from where it's grown to where it's eaten is a bigger culprit as are wastage and war.

Explain TWO reasons why G.M. crops appeal to less developed countries. Also, according to the United Nation World Food Program, what are the primary reasons for food shortages among developing countries?

NOTE

Step 1	Survey
Key Words	
Signal Words	
Step 2	**Reading**
Purpose	
Pattern of Organization	
Tone	
Main Idea	
Step 3	**Summary**
지문 요약하기 (Paraphrasing)	
Step 4	**Recite**
요약문 말로 설명하기	

04 **Read the passage and follow the directions.** [4 points]

Benjamin Blencowe and his team have recently uncovered how a small change in a protein called PTBP1 can spur the creation of neurons—cells that make the brain—that could have fuelled the evolution of mammalian brains to become the largest and most complex among vertebrates.

Brain size and complexity vary enormously across vertebrates, but it is not clear how these differences came about. Humans and frogs, for example, have been evolving separately for 350 million years and have very different brain abilities. Yet scientists have shown that they use a remarkably similar repertoire of genes to build organs in the body.

So how is it that a similar number of genes, that are also switched on or off in similar ways in diverse vertebrate species, generate a vast range of organ size and complexity?

The key lays in the process that Blencowe's group studies, known as alternative splicing (AS), whereby gene products are assembled into proteins, which are the building blocks of life. During AS, gene fragments —called exons—are shuffled to make different protein shapes. It's like LEGO, where some fragments can be missing from the final protein shape.

AS enables cells to make more than one protein from a single gene, so that the total number of different proteins in a cell greatly surpasses the number of available genes. A cell's ability to regulate protein diversity at any given time reflects its ability to take on different roles in the body. AS prevalence increases with vertebrate complexity. So although the genes that make bodies of vertebrates might be similar, the proteins they give rise to are far more diverse in animals such as mammals, than in birds and frogs. And nowhere is AS more widespread than in the brain.

Describe what alternative splicing is and explain why it could be the key to how human beings evolved to become the smartest animal on the planet.

NOTE

Step 1	Survey
Key Words	
Signal Words	
Step 2	**Reading**
Purpose	
Pattern of Organization	
Tone	
Main Idea	
Step 3	**Summary**
지문 요약하기 (Paraphrasing)	
Step 4	**Recite**
요약문 말로 설명하기	

05 **Read the passage and follow the directions.** [4 points]

Two traits that set humans apart from other primates—big brains and the ability to walk upright—could be at odds when it comes to childbirth. Big brains and the big heads that encase them are hard to push through the human birth canal, but a wider pelvis might compromise bipedal walking. Scientists have long posited that nature's solution to this problem, which is known as the "obstetric dilemma," was to shorten the duration of gestation so that babies are born before their heads get too big. As a result, human babies are relatively helpless and seemingly underdeveloped in terms of motor and cognitive ability compared to other primates.

All these fascinating phenomena in human evolution—bipedalism, difficult childbirth, wide female hips, big brains, relatively helpless babies—have traditionally been tied together with the obstetric dilemma. It's been taught in anthropology courses for decades, but when I looked for hard evidence that it's actually true, I struck out.

The problem with the theory is that there is no evidence that hips wide enough to deliver a more developed baby would be a detriment to walking. That throws doubt on the assumption that the size of the birth canal is limited by bipedalism. Wide hips don't mean you can't walk efficiently. Controlling for mother's body size, human gestation is a bit longer than expected compared to other primates, not shorter. And babies are a bit larger than expected, not smaller. Although babies behave like it, they're not born early.

For mammals in general, including humans, gestation length and offspring size are predicted by mother's body size. Because body size is a good proxy for an animal's metabolic rate and function, metabolism might offer a better explanation for the timing of human birth than the pelvis. Women give birth just as they are about to cross into a metabolic danger zone. During pregnancy, women approach that energetic ceiling and give birth right before they reach it. That suggests there is an energetic limit to human gestation length and fetal growth. Those metabolic constraints help explain why human babies are so helpless compared to our primate kin, like chimpanzees. A chimp baby begins crawling at one month, whereas human babies don't crawl until around seven months. But for a human to give birth to a newborn at the same developmental level as chimp, it would take a 16-month gestation. That would place mothers well past their energetic limits. In fact, even one extra month of gestation would cross into the metabolic danger zone.

**bipedalism: walking on two legs*

The writer of the passage refutes long-held theory on human gestation. First, describe what the long-held theory is. Second, according to the author, why are human babies relatively helpless and underdeveloped compared to other primates? When you answer, do NOT copy more than FIVE consecutive words from the passage.

NOTE

Step 1	Survey
Key Words	
Signal Words	
Step 2	**Reading**
Purpose	
Pattern of Organization	
Tone	
Main Idea	
Step 3	**Summary**
지문 요약하기 (Paraphrasing)	
Step 4	**Recite**
요약문 말로 설명하기	

MEMO

06 **Read the passage and follow the directions.** [4 points]

With the rise of the great metropolis in the industrial era, city planning in the West passed out of the hands of the architect and into the hands of the technocrat. Unlike the architect who thought of the city as a work of art to be built up with an eye toward beauty, the technocrat has always taken a purely functional approach to city planning: the city exists for the sole purpose of serving the needs of its inhabitants. Its outward appearance has no intrinsic value.

Over the span of a few centuries, this new breed of urban planner has succeeded in forever changing the face of the Western city. A brief visit to any large metropolis is enough to confirm this grim fact. Even a casual observer could not fail to notice that the typical urban landscape is arranged along the lines of the tedious chessboard pattern, with its fourcornered intersections and long, straight and dull streets. Strict building codes have resulted in an overabundance of unsightly neighborhoods in which there is only slight variation among structures. Rows of squat concrete apartment houses and files of gigantic steel and glass skyscrapers have almost completely replaced older, more personal buildings. Moreover, the lovely natural surroundings of many cities are no longer a part of the urban landscape. For the most part, the hills and rivers which were once so much a part of so many metropolitan settings have now been blotted out by primarily _____①_____ construction.

The lone bright spot amidst all of this urban blight has been the local park system, which is to be found in most Western cities. Large, centrally-located parks—for example, New York's Central Park or London's Hyde Park—and smaller, outlying parks bring a measure of beauty to Western cities by breaking up the man-made monotony. With their green pastures, dense woods, and pleasant ponds, streams and waterfalls, local park systems also offer a vast array of opportunities for city dwellers to rest or recreate, free of the intense burdens of urban life. If they have understood nothing else about the quality of life in urban areas, technocrats have at least had ② <u>the good sense to recognize</u> that people need a quiet refuge from the chaotic bustle of the city.

The writer of the passage, in the first paragraph, contrasts architects to technocrats. Explain this difference in ONE sentence. Second, what does the underlined part suggest about technocrats? Write your answer in 10 words or so. When you answer the questions, do NOT copy more than FIVE consecutive words from the passage. Third, fill in the blank with ONE most appropriate word from the passage.

____

____

____

____

____

NOTE

Step 1	Survey
Key Words	
Signal Words	
Step 2	**Reading**
Purpose	
Pattern of Organization	
Tone	
Main Idea	
Step 3	**Summary**
지문 요약하기 (Paraphrasing)	
Step 4	**Recite**
요약문 말로 설명하기	

07 **Read the passage and follow the directions.** [4 points]

The line between a prejudiced belief and a merely controversial one is elusive, and the harder you look the more elusive it becomes. "God hates homosexuals" is a statement of fact, not of bias, to those who believe it; "American criminals are disproportionately black" is a statement of bias, not of fact, to those who disbelieve it. Who is right? You may decide, and so may others, and there is no need to agree. That is the great innovation of ____________. We cannot know in advance or for sure which belief is prejudice and which is truth, but to advance knowledge we don't need to know. The genius of intellectual pluralism lies not in doing away with prejudices and dogmas but in channeling them—making them socially productive by pitting prejudice against prejudice and dogma against dogma, exposing all to withering public criticism. What survives at the end of the day is our base of knowledge.

Fill in the blank with the TWO most appropriate word from the passage. Second, outline the writer's reason for defending prejudice.

NOTE

Step 1	Survey
Key Words	
Signal Words	
Step 2	**Reading**
Purpose	
Pattern of Organization	
Tone	
Main Idea	
Step 3	**Summary**
지문 요약하기 (Paraphrasing)	
Step 4	**Recite**
요약문 말로 설명하기	

08 **Read the passage and follow the directions.** [4 points]

The lives of insects, at the broadest level, are organized to produce the greatest number of offspring that are mature and successful. This number defines an insect's fitness. There are many ways to maximize fitness, but they all involve economizing time and energy, the common currencies of life. Time and energy budgets are shaped, evolutionarily, according to the principles of stringency and allocation. This means that the budgets are geared to fit the worst conditions an insect might encounter and that time and energy are allocated among survival and reproductive activities so as to maximize fitness. Each sex of an insect species typically allocates a certain portion of its time carrying out several necessary activities, such as feeding, nest making, mating, grooming, and quiescence. Quiescence serves to avoid natural enemies, inimical weather, or stressful times of day, while important internal activities continue, such as food digestion. The energy obtained by feeding is likewise budgeted among several activities that compete for energy use, such as metabolic activity, formation of sperm or eggs, locomotion, and behaviors for obtaining specific nutrients, finding mates, and defense. The best budgets are those that lead to the largest ____________ and become propagated through natural selection. Thus we assume that the way insects organize and distribute their behaviors is roughly optimized for a particular insect niche.

Write the THREE most appropriate consecutive words from the passage that best fit in the blank. Second, explain the importance of quiescence in an insect's energy budget as described in the passage.

NOTE

Step 1	Survey
Key Words	
Signal Words	
Step 2	**Reading**
Purpose	
Pattern of Organization	
Tone	
Main Idea	
Step 3	**Summary**
지문 요약하기 (Paraphrasing)	
Step 4	**Recite**
요약문 말로 설명하기	

09 **Read the passage and follow the directions.** [4 points]

It has long been assumed that cultural bias in assigning and reinforcing gender roles has led to an unfair characterization of women as more apt to complain and less able to bear pain. Boys are raised in many places not to show pain, but instead, as an exhibition of strength, to remain passive before it. Recent research suggests, however, that men and women actually experience pain differently. It has long been known, for instance, that men and women each prefer different classes of painkillers and that these painkillers morphine and nalbuphine treat two different parts of the brain. It has also been shown that babies show different responses to pain within six hours of birth, and that rats and mice have clear gender differences in how they respond to the same stimuli.

The most recent research shows that not only are migraines three times more common in women than men, but that it might be associated with a lowered pain threshold but only in women. A Canadian geneticist who conducted part of this research also isolated a gene that, in women, affects their sensitivity to and ability to tolerate pain. It had no effect on men. He now believes that male and female brains actually process painful stimuli using wholly different sets of neurons and neurotransmitters. In conjunction with the other evidence and well-known surveys showing that women report feeling more pain, more frequently in more parts of their body and for longer periods than men, it might not simply be cultural bias but actual genetics that dictates that "<u>boys don't cry</u>."

In the above passage, explain the key evidence used to argue that both sexes experience pain differently. Then, explain the meaning of the underlined expression.

NOTE

Step 1	Survey
Key Words	
Signal Words	
Step 2	**Reading**
Purpose	
Pattern of Organization	
Tone	
Main Idea	
Step 3	**Summary**
지문 요약하기 (Paraphrasing)	
Step 4	**Recite**
요약문 말로 설명하기	

10 **Read the passage and follow the directions.** [4 points]

Mohammad Yunus of Bangladesh, founder of the Grameen Bank and the main inventor of microcredit schemes, didn't start off with the goal of giving poor people credit. Initially he started off with the conviction that the Green Revolution, and irrigation, was the answer to poverty in Bangladesh. His doctoral dissertation at Vanderbilt University was titled "Optimal Allocation of Multi-Purpose Reservoir Water: A Dynamic Programming Model." His first attempt to help the poor was to sponsor tube wells for irrigation during the dry season so farmers could grow two crops a year. Yunus gave the farmers a loan out of his own money to finance the scheme. The farmers reaped a good harvest. Ironically for the founder of the idea that the poor can be a good credit risk, the farmers didn't fully repay Yunus, and he lost money.

Yunus persisted, visiting as many rural villages as possible to try to understand how to help. He then encountered a woman named Sufiya Begum making a bamboo stool. Begum made a pitiful two cents on every stool, mainly because a moneylender charged her a very high interest rate to advance her the bamboo. Yunus realized that very small loans to very poor people could make a big difference in their lives. He experimented, and found that microcredit borrowers would repay the loan in order to get access to future loans. His first loan at the Grameen Bank was to Sufiya, who started a successful peddling business with the money. There was a huge demand for such loans, and the Grameen Bank became the legend that it is today with imitators from all over the world.

Explain the meaning of the underlined "Ironically". Second, describe the way that Yunus incentivized loan payback.

NOTE

Step 1	Survey
Key Words	
Signal Words	
Step 2	**Reading**
Purpose	
Pattern of Organization	
Tone	
Main Idea	
Step 3	**Summary**
지문 요약하기 (Paraphrasing)	
Step 4	**Recite**
요약문 말로 설명하기	

11 **Read the passage and follow the directions.** [4 points]

One kind of _____①_____ deserves special mention. This is the mistake that arises from the misuse of relative terms, which have different meanings in different contexts. For example, the word "tall" is a relative word; a tall man and a tall building are in quite different categories. A tall man is one who is taller than most men; a tall building is one that is taller than most buildings. Certain forms of argument that are valid for nonrelative terms break down when relative terms are substituted for them. The argument "an elephant is an animal; therefore a gray elephant is a gray animal" is perfectly valid. The word "gray" is a nonrelative term. But the argument "an elephant is an animal; therefore a small elephant is a small animal" is ridiculous. The point here is that "small" is a relative term: A small elephant is a very large animal. The fallacy is one of equivocation with regard to the relative term "small". Not all equivocation on relative terms is so obvious, however. The word "good" is a relative term and is frequently equivocated on when it is argued, for example, that so-and-so is a good general and would therefore be a good president, or that ② <u>someone is a good scholar and is therefore likely to be a good teacher.</u>

Fill in the blank with the ONE most appropriate word from the passage. Second, explain what the writer argues by the underlined part in the final sentence.

____

____

____

____

____

NOTE

Step 1	Survey
Key Words	
Signal Words	
Step 2	**Reading**
Purpose	
Pattern of Organization	
Tone	
Main Idea	
Step 3	**Summary**
지문 요약하기 (Paraphrasing)	
Step 4	**Recite**
요약문 말로 설명하기	

12 **Read the passage and follow the directions.** [4 points]

Faith in progress is deep within our American culture. We have been taught to believe that our lives are better than the lives of those who came before us. The ideology of modern economics suggests that material progress has yielded enhanced satisfaction and well-being. But much of our confidence about our own well-being comes from the assumption that our lives are easier than those of earlier generations. I have already disputed the notion that we work less than medieval European peasants, however poor they may have been. The field research of anthropologists gives another view of <u>the conventional wisdom.</u> The lives of so-called primitive peoples are commonly thought to be harsh—their existence dominated by the "incessant quest for food." In fact, primitives do little work. By contemporary standards, we'd have to judge them very lazy. If the Kapauku of Papua work one day, they do no labor on the next. Kung Bushmen put in only two and a half days per week and six hours per day. In the Sandwich Islands of Hawaii, men work only four hours per day. And Australian aborigines have similar schedules. The key to understanding why these "Stone-Age peoples" fail to act like us—increasing their work effort to get more things—is that they have limited desires. In the race between wanting and having, they have kept their wanting low. In this way, they ensure their own kind of satisfaction. They are materially poor by contemporary standards, but in at least one dimension—time—we have to count them richer.

Identify what "the conventional wisdom" is. Also, explain how "Stone-Age peoples" ensures their satisfaction.

NOTE

Step 1	Survey
Key Words	
Signal Words	
Step 2	**Reading**
Purpose	
Pattern of Organization	
Tone	
Main Idea	
Step 3	**Summary**
지문 요약하기 (Paraphrasing)	
Step 4	**Recite**
요약문 말로 설명하기	

13 **Read the passage and follow the directions.** [4 points]

The common belief of some linguists that each language is a ___①___ vehicle for the thoughts of the nation speaking it is in some ways the exact counterpart of the conviction of the Manchester school of economics that supply and demand will regulate everything for the best. Just as economists were blind to the numerous cases in which the law of supply and demand left actual wants unsatisfied, so also many linguists are deaf to those instances in which the very nature of a language calls forth misunderstandings in everyday conversation, and in which, consequently, a word has to be modified or defined in order to present the idea intended by the speaker: ② "He took his stick — no, not John's, but his own." No language is perfect, and if we admit this truth we must also admit that it is not unreasonable to investigate the relative merits of different languages or of different details in languages.

Fill in the blank with the ONE most appropriate word from the passage. Second, what contributes to the misunderstanding described by the author in the underlined part "He took his stick — no, not John's, but his own."?

NOTE

Step 1	Survey
Key Words	
Signal Words	
Step 2	**Reading**
Purpose	
Pattern of Organization	
Tone	
Main Idea	
Step 3	**Summary**
지문 요약하기 (Paraphrasing)	
Step 4	**Recite**
요약문 말로 설명하기	

14 **Read the passage and follow the directions.** [4 points]

When I was teaching English at the Colorado Rocky Mountain School, I used to ask my students the kinds of questions that English teachers usually ask about reading assignments—questions designed to bring out the points that I had decided they should know. They, on their part, would try to get me to give them hints and clues as to what I wanted. It was a game of wits. I never gave my students an opportunity to say what they really thought about a book. I gave vocabulary drills and quizzes too. I told my students that every time they came upon a word in their book they did not understand, they were to look it up in the dictionary. I even devised special kinds of vocabulary tests, allowing them to use their books to see how the words were used. But looking back, I realize that ① these tests, along with many of my methods, were foolish. My sister was the first person who made me question my conventional ideas about teaching English. She had a son in the seventh grade in a fairly good public school. His teacher had asked the class to read Cooper's *The Deerslayer*. The choice was bad enough in itself; whether looking at man or nature, Cooper was superficial, inaccurate and sentimental, and his writing is ponderous and ornate. But to make matters worse, this teacher had decided to give the book the microscope and X-ray treatment. He made the students look up and memorize not only the definitions but the derivations of every big word that came along—and there were plenty. Every chapter was followed by close questioning and testing to make sure the students "understood" everything. Being then, as I said, _____②_____, I began to defend the teacher, who was a good friend of mine, against my sister's criticisms. The argument soon grew hot. What was wrong with making sure that children understood everything they read? My sister answered that until this year her boy had always loved reading, and had read a lot on his own; now he had stopped. He was not really to start again for many years.

Explain the reason the writer thinks the underlined "these tests" were unwise. Second, fill in the blank with the ONE most appropriate word from the passage.

NOTE

Step 1	Survey
Key Words	
Signal Words	
Step 2	**Reading**
Purpose	
Pattern of Organization	
Tone	
Main Idea	
Step 3	**Summary**
지문 요약하기 (Paraphrasing)	
Step 4	**Recite**
요약문 말로 설명하기	

15 **Read the passage and follow the directions.** [4 points]

It is very easy to argue that ① knowledge about Shakespeare or Wordsworth is not political whereas knowledge about contemporary China or North Korea is. My own formal and professional designation is that of "humanist", a title which indicates the humanities as my field and therefore the unlikely eventuality that there might be anything political about what I do in that field. Of course, all these labels and terms are quite unnuanced as I use them here, but the general truth of what I am pointing to is widely held. One reason for saying that a humanist who writes about Wordsworth or an editor whose specialty is Keats is not involved in anything political is that what he does seems to have no direct political effect upon reality in the everyday sense. A scholar whose field is Chinese economics works in a highly charged area where there is much government interest, and what he might produce in the way of studies or proposals will be taken up by policymakers, government officials, institutional economists, intelligence experts. The distinction between "humanists" and persons whose work has policy implications, or political significance, can be broadened further by saying that the former's ideological color is a matter of incidental importance to politics, whereas the ideology of the latter is woven directly into his material—indeed, economics, politics, and sociology in the modern academy are ideological sciences—and therefore taken for granted as being "political."

Nevertheless, the determining impingement on most knowledge produced in the contemporary West is that it be nonpolitical, that is, scholarly, academic, impartial, above partisan or small-minded doctrinal belief. One can have no quarrel with such an ambition in theory, perhaps, but in practice the reality is much more problematic. No one has ever devised a method for detaching the scholar from the circumstances of life, from the fact of his involvement (conscious or unconscious) with a class, a set of beliefs, a social position, or from the mere activity of being a member of a society. These continue to bear on what he does professionally, even though naturally enough his research and its fruits do attempt to reach a level of relative freedom from the inhibitions and the restrictions of brute, everyday reality. For there is such a thing as knowledge that is less, rather than more, partial than the individual (with his entangling and distracting life circumstances) who produces it. Yet this knowledge is not therefore automatically ______②______.

What is the writer's opinion about the argument expressed in the underlined words in ①? Do not copy more than SIX consecutive words from the passage. Second, fill in the blank with the ONE most appropriate word from the passage.

____

____

____

____

____

NOTE

Step 1	Survey
Key Words	
Signal Words	
Step 2	**Reading**
Purpose	
Pattern of Organization	
Tone	
Main Idea	
Step 3	**Summary**
지문 요약하기 (Paraphrasing)	
Step 4	**Recite**
요약문 말로 설명하기	

MEMO

16 **Read the passage and follow the directions.** [4 points]

Love of money has been denounced by moralists since the world began. I do not wish to add another to the moral denunciations, of which the efficacy in the past has not been encouraging. I wish to show how the worship of money is both an effect and a cause of diminishing vitality and how our institutions might be changed so as to make the worship of money grow less and the general vitality grow more. It is not the desire for money as a means to definite ends that is in question. A struggling artist may desire money in order to have leisure for his art, but this desire is finite and can be satisfied fully by a very modest sum. It is the worship of money that I wish to consider: the belief that all values may be measured in terms of money, and that money is the ultimate test of success in life. This belief is held in fact, if not in words, by multitudes of men and women, and yet it is not in harmony with human nature, since it ignores vital needs and the instinctive tendency towards some specific kind of growth. It makes men treat as unimportant those of their desires which run counter to the acquisition of money, and yet such desires are, as a rule, more important to well-being than any increase of income. It leads men to mutilate their own natures from a mistaken theory of what constitutes success, and to admire enterprises that add nothing to human welfare. It promotes a dead uniformity of character and purpose, a diminution in the joy of life, and a stress and strain which leaves whole communities weary, discouraged, and disillusioned.

Describe the writer's opinion about the moralists' denunciations. Second, identify what the worship of money disregards.

NOTE

Step 1	Survey
Key Words	
Signal Words	
Step 2	**Reading**
Purpose	
Pattern of Organization	
Tone	
Main Idea	
Step 3	**Summary**
지문 요약하기 (Paraphrasing)	
Step 4	**Recite**
요약문 말로 설명하기	

17 **Read the passage and follow the directions.** [3 points]

Sometimes such innovators are of a sombre sincerity, like Tolstoi, sometimes of a sensitive and feminine eloquence, like Nietzsche. In those cases they make a stir and perhaps found a school. It is always supposed that the man in question has discovered a new idea, but, in fact what is new is not the idea, but only the isolation of the idea.

In case this point is not clear, I will take one example, in reference to notions fashionable among some of the more fanciful and younger theorists. Nietzsche, as everyone knows, preached a doctrine which he and his followers regard apparently as very revolutionary: he held that ordinary altruistic morality had been the invention of a slave class to prevent the emergence of superior types to fight and rule them. Now, modern people, whether they agree with this or not, always talk of it as a new and unheard-of idea. It is calmly and persistently supposed that the great writers of the past, say Shakespeare for instance, did not hold this view, because they had never imagined it, because it had never come into their heads. Turn to the last act of Shakespeare's *Richard III* and you will find not only all that Nietzsche had to say put into two lines, but you will find it put in the very words of Nietzsche. Richard Crookback says to his nobles: *Conscience is but a word that cowards use,/ Devised at first to keep the strong in awe.*

As I have said, the fact is plain. Shakespeare had thought of Nietzsche and the master morality, but he weighed it at its proper value and put it in its proper place. Its proper place is the mouth of a half-insane hunchback on the eve of defeat. This rage against the weak is only possible in a man morbidly brave but fundamentally sick: a man like Richard, a man like Nietzsche. This case alone ought to destroy the absurd fancy that these modern philosophies are modern in the sense that the great men of the past did not think of them. They thought of them; only they did not think much of them. It was not that Shakespeare did not see the Nietzsche idea; he saw it, and he saw through it.

State the main idea of the passage. Write down your answer in 30-40 words.

NOTE

Step 1	Survey
Key Words	
Signal Words	
Step 2	**Reading**
Purpose	
Pattern of Organization	
Tone	
Main Idea	
Step 3	**Summary**
지문 요약하기 (Paraphrasing)	
Step 4	**Recite**
요약문 말로 설명하기	

18 **Read the passage and follow the directions.** [4 points]

Here is one widely-regarded reason to worry about the growing inequality of American life: Too great a gap between rich and poor undermines the solidarity that democratic citizenship requires. Here's how: as inequality deepens, rich and poor live increasingly separate lives. The affluent send their children to private schools (or to public schools in wealthy suburbs), leaving urban public schools to the children of families who have no alternative. A similar trend leads to the secession by the privileged from other public institutions and facilities. Private health clubs replace municipal recreation centers and swimming pools. Upscale residential communities hire private security guards and rely less on public police protection. A second or third car removes the need to rely on public transportation. And so on. The affluent secede from public places and services, leaving them to those who can't afford anything else.

This has two bad effects, one fiscal, the other civic. First, public services deteriorate, as those who no longer use those services become less willing to support them with their taxes. Second, public institutions such as schools, parks, playgrounds, and community centers cease to be places where citizens from different walks of life encounter one another. Institutions that once gathered people together and served as informal schools of civic virtue become few and far between. The hollowing out of the public realm makes it difficult to cultivate the solidarity and sense of community on which democratic citizenship depends.

If the erosion of the public realm is the problem, what is the solution? A politics of the common good would take as one of its primary goals the reconstruction of the infrastructure of civic life. Rather than focus on redistribution for the sake of broadening access to private consumption, it would tax the affluent to rebuild public institutions and services so that rich and poor alike would want to take advantage of them.

An earlier generation made a massive investment in the federal highway program, which gave Americans unprecedented individual mobility and freedom, but also contributed to the reliance on the private automobile, suburban sprawl, environmental degradation, and living patterns corrosive to community. This generation could commit itself to an equally consequential investment in an infrastructure for civic renewal: public schools to which rich and poor alike would want to send their children; public transportation systems reliable enough to attract upscale commuters; and public health clinics, playgrounds, parks, recreation centers, libraries, and museums that would, ideally at least, draw people out of their gated communities and into the common spaces of a shared democratic citizenship.

Identify the negative effects of the diminution of public institutions. Second, describe the specific solution to the erosion of the public realm proffered by the writer.

NOTE

Step 1	Survey
Key Words	
Signal Words	
Step 2	**Reading**
Purpose	
Pattern of Organization	
Tone	
Main Idea	
Step 3	**Summary**
지문 요약하기 (Paraphrasing)	
Step 4	**Recite**
요약문 말로 설명하기	

MEMO

19 **Read the passage and follow the directions.** [4 points]

When he graduated from university with a degree in ethnic studies, Anthony found a solid job in his profession, married, and had two sons, Sammy and Tony. Twelve years later, he moved to another company that promised steady advancement within its managerial ranks. A devoted family man, he admired his wife Lauren's dedication to raising the boys. But he also observed that his sons, approaching their teen years, benefited greatly from his fatherly friendship and counsel—especially as they approached what he and his wife realized could prove to be a difficult transitional period in their upbringing. So he made a commitment to spend plenty of time with them, playing baseball and helping with their schoolwork.

But he also loved his work and did well at it, and it quickly became apparent that, to advance rapidly up the ____________, he needed a master's degree. A nearby university offered the degree in an attractive evening-and-weekend program that would allow him to continue full-time employment. But it would soak up the next several years of his life and throw most of the family activities into his wife's hands. Anthony's dilemma set the short-term goals against the long-term ones. It was right, he felt, to honor his family's short-term needs to take care of his sons. Yet it was right to build for the long-term needs of his family.

Explain both the short-term needs and the long term needs of Anthony's family in your own words. Do not copy more than FIVE consecutive words from the passage. Second, fill in the blank with the TWO consecutive words from the passage.

NOTE

Step 1	Survey
Key Words	
Signal Words	
Step 2	**Reading**
Purpose	
Pattern of Organization	
Tone	
Main Idea	
Step 3	**Summary**
지문 요약하기 (Paraphrasing)	
Step 4	**Recite**
요약문 말로 설명하기	

20 **Read the passage and follow the directions.** [4 points]

Zoos were originally created as places of entertainment, and their suggested involvement with conservation didn't seriously arise until about 40 years ago, when the Zoological Society of London held the first formal international meeting on the subject. Eight years later, a series of world conferences took place, entitled "The Breeding of Endangered Species," and from this point onwards conservation became the zoo community's buzzword. This commitment has now been clearly defined in The World Zoo Conservation Strategy (WZCS). However, the important and welcome document is based on an unrealistic optimism about the nature of the zoo industry.

The WZCS estimates that there are about 10,000 zoos in the world, of which around 1,000 represent a core of quality collections capable of participating in co-ordinated conservation programmes. This is the document's first failing, as I believe that 10,000 is a serious underestimate of the total number of places masquerading as zoological establishments. Of course it is difficult to get accurate data but, to put the issue into perspective, I have found that, in a year of working in Eastern Europe, I discover fresh zoos on almost a weekly basis.

The second flaw in the reasoning of the WZCS document is the naive faith it places in its 1,000 core zoos. One would assume that the calibre of these institutions would have been carefully examined, but it appears that the criterion for inclusion on this select list is that the zoo is a member of a zoo federation or association. This might be a good starting point, working on the premise that members must meet certain standards, but again the facts don't support the theory. The greatly respected American Association of Zoological Parks and Aquariums has had extremely dubious members, and the Federation of Zoological Gardens of Great Britain and Ireland has occasionally had members that have been roundly censured in the national press. These include Robin Hill Adventure Park on the Isle of Wight, which many considered the most notorious collection of animals in the country.

Identify the goal and the two defects of the WZCS document. Then, explain the reason the writer mentions Robin Hill Adventure Park. Do not copy more than FIVE consecutive words from the passage.

NOTE

Step 1	Survey
Key Words	
Signal Words	
Step 2	**Reading**
Purpose	
Pattern of Organization	
Tone	
Main Idea	
Step 3	**Summary**
지문 요약하기 (Paraphrasing)	
Step 4	**Recite**
요약문 말로 설명하기	

21 **Read the passage and follow the directions.** [4 points]

The nineteenth century suffered from a curious division between its political ideas and its economic practices. In politics it carried out the liberal ideas of Locke and Rousseau, which were adapted to a society of small peasant proprietors. Its watchwords were *liberty* and *equality*, but meanwhile it was inventing the technique which is leading the twentieth century to destroy liberty and to replace equality by new forms of oligarchy. The prevalence of liberal thought has been in some ways a misfortune, since it has prevented men of large vision from thinking out in an impersonal manner the problems raised by industrialism. Socialism and Communism, it is true, are essentially industrial creeds, but their outlook is so dominated by the class war that they have little leisure to give to anything but the means of achieving political victory. Traditional morality gives very little help in the modern world. A rich man may plunge millions into destitution by some act which not even the severest Catholic confessor would consider sinful, while he will need absolution for a trivial sexual aberration which, at the worst, has wasted an hour that might have been more usefully employed. There is need of a new doctrine on the subject of my duty to my neighbor. It is not only traditional religious teaching that fails to give adequate guidance on this subject, but also the teaching of nineteenth-century liberalism. Take, for example, Stuart Mill on liberty. Mill maintains that while the state has a right to interfere with those of my actions that have serious consequences to others, it should leave me free where the effects of my actions are mainly confined to myself. Such a principle, however, in the modern world, leaves hardly any scope for individual freedom. As society becomes more organic, the effects of men upon each other become more and more numerous and important, so that there remains hardly anything in regard to which Mill's defense of liberty is applicable.

Describe Stuart Mill's theory on liberty and explain the reason the writer considers Mill's theory to be defective. Do not copy more than SEVEN consecutive words from the passage.

NOTE

Step 1	Survey
Key Words	
Signal Words	
Step 2	**Reading**
Purpose	
Pattern of Organization	
Tone	
Main Idea	
Step 3	**Summary**
지문 요약하기 (Paraphrasing)	
Step 4	**Recite**
요약문 말로 설명하기	

22 **Read the passage and follow the directions.** [4 points]

One of the most infamous incidents in New York City history was the 1964 stabbing death of Kitty Genovese. She was chased by her assailant and attacked three times on the street over the course of half an hour as thirty-eight of her neighbors watched from their windows. During that time, however, none of the thirty eight witnesses called the police. The case provoked rounds of self-recrimination. Abe Rosenthal, who would later become editor of the *New York Times*, wrote that nobody can say why the thirty-eight did not pick up the phone while Miss Genovese was being attacked, since they cannot say themselves. It can be assumed, however, that their apathy was indeed one of the big-city variety. It is almost a matter of psychological survival, if one is surrounded and pressed by millions of people, to prevent them from constantly impinging on you, and the only way to do this is to ignore them as often as possible. Indifference to one's neighbor and his troubles is a conditioned reflex in life in New York as it is in other big cities. This is the kind of environmental explanation that makes intuitive sense to us. The truth about Genovese, however, turns out to be a little more complicated—and more interesting. Two psychologists—Bibb Latane of Columbia University and John Darley of New York University—subsequently conducted a series of studies to try to understand what they dubbed the "bystander problem." They staged emergencies of one kind or another in different situations in order to see who would come and help. What they found was surprising. In one experiment, for example, Latane and Darley had a student alone in a room stage an epileptic fit. When there was just one person next door, listening, that person rushed to the student's aid 85 percent of the time. But when subjects thought that there were four others also overhearing the seizure, they came to the student's aid only 31 percent of the time. In another experiment, people who saw smoke seeping out from under a doorway would report it 75 percent of the time when they were on their own, but the incident would be reported only 38 percent of the time when they were in a group. When people are in a group, in other words, responsibility for acting is diffused. They assume that someone else will make the call, or they assume that because no one else is acting, the apparent problem—the seizure-like sounds from the other room, the smoke from the door — isn't really a problem. Ironically, had she been attacked on a lonely street with just one witness, she might have lived.

What is Abe Rosenthal's explanation of the case of Kitty Genovese? Second, describe what Latane and Darley find.

NOTE

Step 1	Survey
Key Words	
Signal Words	
Step 2	**Reading**
Purpose	
Pattern of Organization	
Tone	
Main Idea	
Step 3	**Summary**
지문 요약하기 (Paraphrasing)	
Step 4	**Recite**
요약문 말로 설명하기	

CHAPTER 02

함축의미, 추론

모범답안 및 번역 p.142

01 **Read the passage and follow the directions.** [4 points]

In Cambridge in the 1920s, F. P. Ramsey single-handedly forged a range of ideas that have since come to define the philosophical landscape. Contemporary debates about truth, meaning, knowledge, logic and the structure of scientific theories all take off from positions first defined by Ramsey. A year before Ramsey died from hepatitis at the age of twenty-six in 1930, Ludwig Wittgenstein returned to Cambridge after his reclusive years in Austria. The cult surrounding Wittgenstein quickly caught fire, and for the next fifty years dominated philosophy throughout the English-speaking world. By the time it subsided, Ramsey had somehow been relegated to a minor role in history.

In some ways, Ramsey and Wittgenstein had much in common. They were both inspired by Russell and saw their initial task in philosophy as improving its account of the relation between language and reality. But they had very different philosophical temperaments. Wittgenstein's first book added a powerful dose of mysticism to his analysis of language, and this gnostic strain became even more pronounced in the neo-idealism of his later philosophy. Ramsey, by contrast, saw the world through the lens of mathematics and fundamental physics. For Wittgenstein, science was an enemy; for Ramsey, it became a friend.

In 1929, Wittgenstein returned to Cambridge for good. He and Ramsey made up their differences and for the best part of a year resumed philosophical discussion. But it is hard to imagine that they would have continued in intellectual harmony for long. Wittgenstein's transcendental hankerings made him impatient with what he saw as Ramsey's materialism. Ramsey for his part was irritated by Wittgenstein's exclusive focus on his own ideas. Over the past century the philosophical landscape has shifted. The central challenge is now to accommodate mind and meaning within the world uncovered by science, and ______________ for some higher perspective have been marginalized. Now it is good to be reminded how far Ramsey went in meeting this challenge.

Write ONE word from the passage that best fills the blank. Additionally, describe what can be inferred regarding the current, relative popularity of Wittgenstein in the shifted philosophical landscape the writer outlines.

____

____

____

____

____

NOTE

Step 1	Survey
Key Words	
Signal Words	
Step 2	**Reading**
Purpose	
Pattern of Organization	
Tone	
Main Idea	
Step 3	**Summary**
지문 요약하기 (Paraphrasing)	
Step 4	**Recite**
요약문 말로 설명하기	

02 **Read the passage and follow the directions.** [4 points]

Five years have passed since the onset of what is sometimes called the Great Recession. While the economy has slowly improved, there are still millions of Americans leading lives of quiet desperation: without jobs, without resources, without hope. Who was to blame? Was it simply a result of negligence, of the kind of inordinate risk-taking commonly called a "bubble," of an imprudent but innocent failure to maintain adequate reserves for a rainy day? Or was it the result, at least in part, of fraudulent practices, of dubious mortgages portrayed as sound risks and packaged into ever more esoteric financial instruments, the fundamental weaknesses of which were intentionally obscured? If it was the former, then the criminal law has no role to play in the aftermath. For in all but a few circumstances, the fierce and fiery weapon called criminal prosecution is directed at intentional misconduct, and nothing less. If the Great Recession was in no part the handiwork of intentionally fraudulent practices by high-level executives, then to prosecute such executives criminally would be "scapegoating" of the most shallow and despicable kind. But if, by contrast, the Great Recession was the product of ______________, the failure to prosecute those responsible must be judged one of the most egregious failures of the criminal justice system in many years. Indeed, it would stand in striking contrast to the increased success that federal prosecutors have had over the past fifty years or so in bringing to justice even the highest-level figures who orchestrated mammoth frauds.

Fill in the blank with the TWO most appropriate consecutive words from the passage. Then, explain what can be inferred regarding the success of prosecution of high-level fraud half a century earlier.

NOTE

Step 1	Survey
Key Words	
Signal Words	
Step 2	**Reading**
Purpose	
Pattern of Organization	
Tone	
Main Idea	
Step 3	**Summary**
지문 요약하기 (Paraphrasing)	
Step 4	**Recite**
	요약문 말로 설명하기

03 **Read the passage and follow the directions.** [4 points]

Cloning and the new technologies of human genetic modification are among the most powerful and consequential technologies ever developed. Two constituencies dominate the current debate over cloning: antiabortion conservatives and biomedical scientists. Many pro-choice feminists worry about a new eugenics that would commodify the process of child-bearing. Human-rights advocates worry that new eugenic technologies would throw fuel on the flames of racial and ethnic hatred. Although both sides support bans on creating cloned children, conservatives also want immediate, permanent bans on the use of cloning techniques that might have research applications, while the biotech industry resists any meaningful regulation whatsoever. It's been suggested as a compromise that Congress enact a ban on creating cloned children while imposing a moratorium, rather than a permanent ban, on research cloning. During a moratorium, the many proposed alternatives to the use of clonal embryos for research could be explored. Unfortunately, neither side has yet been willing to make the first public move towards pragmatic compromises of this sort. To break this deadlock, we need a broader range of constituencies considering the full implications of cloning.

Explain the meaning of the underlined phrase. Second, from the above passage, what can be inferred about the liberal or progressive perspective on biomedical research? Write your answer in no more than TWO sentences. Do not copy more than three consecutive words from the passage.

NOTE

Step 1	Survey
Key Words	
Signal Words	
Step 2	**Reading**
Purpose	
Pattern of Organization	
Tone	
Main Idea	
Step 3	**Summary**
지문 요약하기 (Paraphrasing)	
Step 4	**Recite**
요약문 말로 설명하기	

04 **Read the passage and follow the directions.** [4 points]

In *The Black Swan*, Nassim Taleb introduced the notion of a narrative fallacy to describe how flawed stories of the past shape our views of the world and our expectations for the future. Narrative fallacies arise inevitably from our continuous attempt to make sense of the world. The explanatory stories that people find compelling are simple; are concrete rather than abstract; assign a larger role to talent, stupidity, and intentions than to luck; and focus on a few striking events that happened rather than on the countless events that failed to happen. Taleb suggests that we humans constantly fool ourselves by constructing flimsy accounts of the past and believing they are true. Good stories provide a simple and coherent account of people's actions and intentions. You are always ready to interpret behavior as a manifestation of general propensities and personality traits—causes that you can readily match to effects. The halo effect contributes to coherence, because it inclines us to match our view of all the qualities of a person to our judgement of one attribute that is particularly significant. The halo effect helps keep explanatory narratives simple and coherent by exaggerating the consistency of evaluations : good people do only good things and bad people are all bad. The statement "Hitler loved dogs and little children" is shocking no matter how many times you hear it, because any trace of kindness in someone so evil violates the expectations set up by the halo effect. Inconsistencies reduce the ease of our thoughts and the clarity of our feelings.

Define what the halo effect is in one sentence. Also, what would be the feeling of the reader if a story was consistent in narrative, according to the passage?

NOTE

Step 1	Survey
Key Words	
Signal Words	
Step 2	**Reading**
Purpose	
Pattern of Organization	
Tone	
Main Idea	
Step 3	**Summary**
지문 요약하기 (Paraphrasing)	
Step 4	**Recite**
요약문 말로 설명하기	

05 **Read the passage and follow the directions.** [4 points]

The notion that geniuses such as Shakespeare, Mozart, and Picasso were "gifted" or possessed innate talents is a myth according to a study by a British psychologist. After examining outstanding performances in the arts and sports, Professor Michael Howe and colleagues at Exeter University concluded that excellence is determined by opportunities, encouragement, training, motivation, self-confidence, and—most of all—practice.

The theory—a radical break with traditional beliefs—has been applauded by academics worldwide. It has significant implications for teachers and parents, not least because children who are not thought to be gifted are being denied the encouragement they need to succeed. The authors took as their starting point the "widespread belief that to reach high levels of ability a person must possess an innate potential called talent." They said it was important to establish whether the belief was correct because ① it had social and educational consequences affecting selection procedures and training.

However, studies of accomplished artists and mathematicians, top tennis players and swimmers reported few early signs of promise prior to parental ____②____. No case was found of anyone reaching the highest levels of achievement without devoting thousands of hours to serious training. Even those who were believed to be exceptionally talented—whether in music, mathematics, chess, or sports—required lengthy periods of instruction and practice.

Fill in the blank with the ONE most appropriate word found in the passage. You may change the word form if necessary. You may change the word form if necessary. Explain the meaning of the underlined words in ①.

NOTE

Step 1	Survey
Key Words	
Signal Words	
Step 2	**Reading**
Purpose	
Pattern of Organization	
Tone	
Main Idea	
Step 3	**Summary**
지문 요약하기 (Paraphrasing)	
Step 4	**Recite**
요약문 말로 설명하기	

06 **Read the passage and follow the directions.** [4 points]

After learning a new physical skill, such as riding a bike, it takes six hours to permanently store the memory in the brain. But interrupt the storage process by learning another new skill and that first lesson may be erased, according to research into memory and the mind. "We've shown that time itself is a very powerful component of learning," said Dr. Henry Holcomb, a psychiatrist who heads a Johns Hopkins University group that studies how people remember. "It is not enough to simply practice something. You have to allow time to pass for the brain to encode the new skill." The researchers used a device that measures blood flow in the brain. They concluded it takes five to six hours for the memory of a new skill to move from a temporary storage site in the front of the brain to a permanent storage site at the back. During those six hours, Holcomb said, there is a neural "window of vulnerability" when that ______________ can be easily eroded from memory if the person attempts to learn a second new skill. "If you were performing a piano piece for the first time and then immediately started practicing something else, then that will cause problems in retention of the initial piece that you practiced," Holcomb said. It would be better, he said, if the first practice session were followed by five to six hours of routine activity that required no new learning.

Fill in the blank with TWO consecutive words from the passage. Second, explain the implied important characteristic of the "routine activity" described in the final sentence.

NOTE

Step 1	Survey
Key Words	
Signal Words	
Step 2	**Reading**
Purpose	
Pattern of Organization	
Tone	
Main Idea	
Step 3	**Summary**
지문 요약하기 (Paraphrasing)	
Step 4	**Recite**
요약문 말로 설명하기	

07 **Read the passage and follow the directions.** [4 points]

The separation of space inside homes may vary from culture to culture. In most American homes the layout of rooms reveals the separateness and labeling of space according to ____________—bedroom, living room, dining room, playroom, and so on. This system is in sharp contrast to other cultures where one room in a house may serve several functions. In Japan, homes with sliding walls can change a large room into two small rooms so that a living room can also serve as a bedroom. When a home or a city's design is influenced by another culture, the "native" architecture can be lost or disguised. For example, a French architect was asked to design Chandigarh, the capital city in Punjab, India. He decided to plan the city with centralized shopping centers which required public transportation and movement away from the village centers. Eventually the Indians stopped meeting each other socially in their small neighborhoods. Apparently, the introduction of a non-Indian style of architecture affected some of the cultural and social patterns of those living in the city.

Fill in the blank with the ONE most appropriate word from the passage. Second, explain what type of marketplaces we can infer that Chandigarh had previous to its redesign.

NOTE

Step 1	Survey
Key Words	
Signal Words	
Step 2	**Reading**
Purpose	
Pattern of Organization	
Tone	
Main Idea	
Step 3	**Summary**
지문 요약하기 (Paraphrasing)	
Step 4	**Recite**
요약문 말로 설명하기	

08 **Read the passage and follow the directions.** [4 points]

The wolf prowls through stories as the embodiment of evil. In a way, it is odd that the wolf should be mankind's worst enemy. Bears, which get a far better press, are more dangerous. Disturb a bear and it may turn on you; disturb a wolf and it will run away. Presumably competition explains this ancient hatred. A pack of wolves will happily kill hundreds of sheep in an hour. <u>In communities whose livelihood goes about on four legs, wolves and people are not compatible</u>. This rivalry spawned awful cruelty, and in the early 19th century America, killing wolves was regarded as fine entertainment. Yet around the middle of the 20th century sentiment started to change. First came a shift in conservationist thinking, illustrated by the life and writings of Aldo Leopold, father of the American environmental movement. In the early 20th century environmentalists believed that because predators killed other animals, conservation was best served by killing them. But Mr Leopold righteously grew concerned about the consequences of this campaign. In one of his best-selling environmentalist books, he wrote, "I have watched the face of many a newly wolfless mountain, and seen the south-facing slopes wrinkle with a maze of new deer trails. I have seen every edible bush and seedling browsed, first to anaemic desuetude, and then to death."

Elucidate the meaning of the underlined words. Then, describe the writer's opinion of wolves in ONE sentence.

NOTE

Step 1	Survey
Key Words	
Signal Words	
Step 2	**Reading**
Purpose	
Pattern of Organization	
Tone	
Main Idea	
Step 3	**Summary**
지문 요약하기 (Paraphrasing)	
Step 4	**Recite**
요약문 말로 설명하기	

CHAPTER

03 요지, 목적, 제목

모범답안 및 번역 p.158

01 **Read the passage and follow the directions.** [4 points]

There are plenty of emotional arguments both for and against animal testing, but let's start with the most obvious facts. If you examine the history of medicine, you find that experiments on animals have been an important part of almost every major medical advance. Many cornerstones of medical science—the discovery that blood circulates through our veins, understanding the way lungs work, the discovery of vitamins and hormones—were made this way.

Most of the main advances in medicine itself also depended on animal experiments. In the Fifties, between 2000 and 4000 people each year in the UK were paralyzed or killed by polio but, thanks to the polio vaccine, this number has now dropped to just one or two cases a year. Modern surgery would be impossible without today's anaesthetics. The list goes on: organ transplants, heart surgery, hip replacements, drugs for cancer and asthma—animals played an important part in these medical advances.

Animal experimentation wasn't the only type of research necessary to the medical advances that save human lives. Studies on human volunteers were also essential, and test-tube experiments were vital in many cases. But the history of medicine tells us that animal experiments are essential if we want to deal with the diseases.

This is the dilemma we face. We want to prevent suffering. The crucial issue is how we use animals in research. Modern science has developed humane experimental techniques. It is possible to do animal experiments using methods that the animals don't even notice. The worst these animals have to put up with is living in a cage with regular food and water, with animal keepers and vets looking after them.

The golden rule of laboratory animal welfare is to minimize any pain involved using the principle of the three Rs. First, you reduce the number of animals used in each experiment to the minimum that will give a scientific result. Then, whenever possible, you replace animal experiments with alternatives—that don't use animals but will give equally scientific results. Finally, you refine the animal experiments that you do, so they cause the least possible harm to the animals. If an experiment involves surgery on the animal, give it an anaesthetic. When it comes around, give it painkillers and medicine to fight infection.

What is the main idea of the passage? Write your answer in ONE sentence. Second, describe what the "three Rs" are. When you answer the questions, do NOT copy more than FIVE consecutive words from the passage.

NOTE

Step 1	Survey
Key Words	
Signal Words	
Step 2	**Reading**
Purpose	
Pattern of Organization	
Tone	
Main Idea	
Step 3	**Summary**
지문 요약하기 (Paraphrasing)	
Step 4	**Recite**
요약문 말로 설명하기	

MEMO

02 **Read the passage and follow the directions.** [4 points]

For the sciences, a new theory is the goal and end result of the creative act. Innovative science produces new propositions in terms of which diverse phenomena can be related to one another in more coherent ways. Such phenomena as a brilliant diamond or a nesting bird are relegated to the role of data, serving as the means for formulating or testing a new theory. The goal of highly creative art is very different: the phenomenon itself becomes the direct product of the creative act. Shakespeare's *Hamlet* is not a tract about the behavior of indecisive princes or the uses of political power, nor is Picasso's painting *Guernica* primarily a propositional statement about the Spanish Civil War or the evils of fascism. What highly creative artistic activity produces is not a new generalization that transcends established limits, but rather an aesthetic particular. Aesthetic particulars produced by the highly creative artist extend, in an innovative way, the limits of an existing form, rather than transcend that form. This is not to deny that a highly creative artist sometimes establishes a new principle of organization in the history of an artistic field: the composer Claudio Monteverdi, who created music of the highest aesthetic value, comes to mind. More generally, however, whether or not a composition establishes a new principle in the history of music has little bearing on its aesthetic worth. Because they embody a new principle of organization, some musical works, such as the operas of *the Florentine Camerata*, are of signal historical importance, but few listeners or musicologists would include these among the great works of music. On the other hand, Mozart's *The Marriage of Figaro* is surely among the masterpieces of music, even though its modest innovations are confined to ____________ existing means.

What is the title of the passage? Write your answer in 10 words or less. Second, why does the writer of the passage mention the Florentine Camerata? Write your answer in ONE sentence. Third, fill in the blank with the ONE word from the passage. If necessary, change the word form.

NOTE

Step 1	Survey
Key Words	
Signal Words	
Step 2	**Reading**
Purpose	
Pattern of Organization	
Tone	
Main Idea	
Step 3	**Summary**
지문 요약하기 (Paraphrasing)	
Step 4	**Recite**
요약문 말로 설명하기	

03 **Read the passage and follow the directions.** [4 points]

Evolution has come up with a big innovation. The mammalian hormone oxytocin evolved to play a key role in what makes mammals mammalian. Other newborn animals typically fend for themselves: Crocodiles, for example, are catching insects soon after birth. But mammals develop slowly, and mothers have to feed their newborns. Oxytocin evolved to make this possible, prompting mothers who are nursing to produce more milk as their babies demand it. Evolving the means to nurse the young was only half the battle. You also have to want to take care of them and to invest zillions of calories in generating milk and fending off predators. And you need to be able to recognize your offspring in a crowd, so you don't waste your energy helping others to leave behind copies of their genes. Oxytocin helped to solve <u>both problems</u>. But something truly striking occurred sometime in the past 50,000 years (which is to say, over the last 0.01% of the time during which oxytocin has existed). During that evolutionary blink of an eye, humans embarked on something new, with oxytocin again in a leading role: the domestication of wolves.

How did this occur? Scientists found that modern dogs and their owners secrete oxytocin when they interact with each other. Remarkably, dogs who gaze the most at their humans during interactions had the biggest oxytocin rise—as did their humans. The scientists then spritzed oxytocin (or saline, as a control treatment) up the dogs' noses. The oxytocin caused female dogs to gaze more at their humans whose own oxytocin levels rose as a result. All of this only affected dogs and their owners. Hand-reared wolves and their owners didn't react in the same way to the treatment, and dogs administered oxytocin didn't gaze any longer at humans who weren't familiar to them. In other words, dog and human brains seem to have evolved at lightning speed to co-opt oxytocin for bonding between our species. This sure helps to explain people who use baby talk with their dogs.

What is the main idea of the passage? Write your answer in ONE sentence. Second, identify the underlined "both problems". When you answer this question, do NOT copy more than FIVE consecutive words from the passage.

NOTE

Step 1	Survey
Key Words	
Signal Words	
Step 2	**Reading**
Purpose	
Pattern of Organization	
Tone	
Main Idea	
Step 3	**Summary**
지문 요약하기 (Paraphrasing)	
Step 4	**Recite**
요약문 말로 설명하기	

04 **Read the passage and follow the directions.** [4 points]

For nearly a century, surgical residency had been a period of both intensive experience and increasing responsibility. More recent research has affirmed that approach, demonstrating the strong link between a surgeon's operative skill, the number of operations performed and patient outcomes. For the past decade, with limits set on their time at the hospital, young surgeons-in-training had fewer opportunities to scrub in on operations. While previous generations of trainees participated in at least one operation a day, new trainees had only enough time to be involved in two or maybe three operations each week. Calculating the number of hours "lost" by cutting back on in-hospital time, surgical leaders estimated that young surgeons-to-be were now missing out on as much as a year's worth of experience. Surgery itself was also changing, and the number of skills surgeons now needed was expanding. The discovery of new medications rendered once standard operations less common, but not entirely obsolete; so surgeons still had to know how to perform all the operations without getting to practice them as often. Surgical training programs scrambled to make up for less time and cover the ever-expanding body of knowledge by creating online educational tools and offering trainees experiences in simulated operating rooms and trauma resuscitations using electronic mannequins. But as a study reveals, even the best-equipped simulation labs cannot replace a year's worth of lost experience.

Explain the writer's main purpose for writing the passage. Additionally, according to the writer, how often should a surgeon in a residency participate in an operation to be trained best?

NOTE

Step 1	Survey
Key Words	
Signal Words	
Step 2	**Reading**
Purpose	
Pattern of Organization	
Tone	
Main Idea	
Step 3	**Summary**
지문 요약하기 (Paraphrasing)	
Step 4	**Recite**
요약문 말로 설명하기	

05 **Read the passage and follow the directions.** [4 points]

The broadcast and print media regularly provide hype for individuals who have achieved "super" success. These stories are usually about celebrities and superstars from the sports and entertainment world. Society pages and gossip columns serve to keep the social elite informed of each other's doings, allow the rest of us to gawk at their excesses, and help to keep the American dream alive. The print media are also fond of feature stories on corporate empire builders. These stories provide an occasional "insider's" view of the private and corporate life of industrialists by suggesting a "rags to riches" account of corporate success. These stories tell us that corporate success is a series of smart moves, shrewd acquisitions, timely mergers, and well-thought-out executive suite shuffles. By painting the upper class in a positive light, innocent of any wrongdoing (labor leaders and union organizations usually get the opposite treatment), the ____________ assure us that wealth and power are benevolent. One person's capital accumulation is presumed to be good for all. The elite, then, are portrayed as investment wizards, people of special talent and skill, whom even their victims (workers and consumers) can admire.

What is the writer's purpose in the passage? Write your answer in about 10 words. Second, fill in the blank with ONE word from the passage.

NOTE

Step 1	Survey
Key Words	
Signal Words	
Step 2	**Reading**
Purpose	
Pattern of Organization	
Tone	
Main Idea	
Step 3	**Summary**
지문 요약하기 (Paraphrasing)	
Step 4	**Recite**
요약문 말로 설명하기	

06 **Read the passage and follow the directions.** [4 points]

After more than forty years of running on parallel tracks, the information and life sciences are beginning to fuse into a single powerful technological and economic force that is laying the foundation for the Biotech Century. The computer is increasingly being used to decipher, manage and organize the vast genetic information that is the raw resource of the new global economy. Already, transnational corporations are creating giant life-science complexes from which to fashion a ____________ world.

Food and fiber will likely be grown indoors in giant bacteria baths, partially eliminating the farmer and the soil for the first time in history. Animal and human cloning could be commonplace, with "replication" increasingly replacing "reproduction." Millions of people could obtain a detailed genetic readout of themselves, allowing them to gaze into their own biological future and predict and plan their lives in ways never before possible. Parents may choose to have their children conceived in test-tubes and gestated in artificial wombs outside the human body. Genetic changes could be made in human fetuses to correct deadly diseases and disorders and enhance mood, behavior, intelligence and physical traits.

The Biotech Century promises a cornucopia of genetically engineered plants and animals to feed a hungry world, genetically derived sources of energy and fiber to propel commerce and build a "renewable" society, wonder drugs and genetic therapies to produce healthier babies, eliminate human suffering, and extend the human life span. But, with every step we take into this "Brave New World," the nagging question, "At what cost?" will haunt us. Will the artificial creation of cloned, chimeric, and transgenic animals mean the end of nature and the substitution of a bio-industrial world? Will the mass release of thousands of generically engineered life forms into the environment cause catastrophic genetic pollution and irreversible damage to the biosphere? What are the consequences—for both the global economy and society—of reducing the world's gene pool to patented intellectual property controlled exclusively by a handful of life-science corporations? What will it mean to live in a world where babies are genetically engineered and customized in the womb, and where people are increasingly identified, stereotyped, and discriminated against on the basis of their genotype? What are the risks we take in attempting to design more "perfect" human beings?

What is the main idea of the passage. Write down your answer in about 30 words. Second, fill in the blank with the ONE most appropriate word from the passage.

NOTE

Step 1	Survey
Key Words	
Signal Words	
Step 2	**Reading**
Purpose	
Pattern of Organization	
Tone	
Main Idea	
Step 3	**Summary**
지문 요약하기 (Paraphrasing)	
Step 4	**Recite**
요약문 말로 설명하기	

04 지칭추론

모범답안 및 번역 p.170

01 **Read the passage and follow the directions.** [4 points]

To begin with, all the standard arguments about why the brain might not be a computer are pretty weak. Take the argument that "brains are parallel, but computers are serial." Critics are right to note that virtually every time a human does anything, many different parts of the brain are engaged; that's parallel, not serial.

But the idea that computers are strictly serial is woefully out of date. Ever since desktop computers became popular, there has always been some degree of parallelism in computers, with several different computations being performed simultaneously, by different components, such as the hard-drive controller and the central processor. And the trend over time in the hardware business has been to make computers more and more parallel, using new approaches like multicore processors and graphics processing units.

Skeptics of the computer metaphor also like to argue that "brains are analog, while computers are digital." The idea here is that things that are digital operate only with discrete divisions, as with a digital watch; things that are analog, like an old-fashioned watch, work on a smooth continuum. But just as either format is possible for a watch, either format is possible for a(n) _____________, and many "digital" computer switches are built out of analog components and processes. Although virtually all modern computers are digital, most early computers were analog. And we still don't really know whether our brains are analog or digital or some mix of the two.

Also, there is a popular argument that human brains are capable of generating emotions, whereas computers are not. But while computers as we know them clearly lack emotions, that fact itself doesn't mean that emotions aren't the product of computation. On the contrary, neural systems like the amygdala that modulate emotions appear to work in roughly the same way as the rest of the brain does, which is to say that they transmit signals and integrate information, and transform inputs into outputs. As any computer scientist will tell you, that's pretty much what computers do.

In the passage, there are three sorts of skeptics, whom the writer of the passage argues against. What are those skeptics' ideas and what does the writer argue against them? Do NOT copy more than FIVE consecutive words from the passage. Second, fill in the blank with the ONE most appropriate word from the passage.

NOTE

Step 1	Survey
Key Words	
Signal Words	
Step 2	**Reading**
Purpose	
Pattern of Organization	
Tone	
Main Idea	
Step 3	**Summary**
지문 요약하기 (Paraphrasing)	
Step 4	**Recite**
요약문 말로 설명하기	

MEMO

02 **Read the passage and follow the directions.** [4 points]

We all have our favourite movie moments, ones we love to watch again from time to time. Chimpanzees and bonobos, too, have the nous to recall thrilling scenes in movies they have previously seen and anticipate when they are about to come up. Apes can readily recall and anticipate significant recent events, just by watching those events once. Rather than use hidden food as a memory test, Japanese researchers made short movies and showed them to apes on two consecutive days.

Kano and his colleague Satoshi Hirata made and starred in two short films. Another of the characters was a human dressed up as an ape in a King Kong costume who carried out attacks on people, providing the key plot moment in the first movie. Both films were designed to contain memorable dramatic events, and the researchers deployed laser eye-tracking technology to see if the animals preferentially noticed and remembered these moments.

The researchers hoped that enacting an emotionally charged scene involving aggression would help them tease out any inklings of memory. In the first of the two 30-second-long movies, the ape character bursts in through the door on the right—one of two visible on screen—and attacks one of the two people 18 seconds in.

Through tracking the gaze of six chimpanzees and six bonobos, the researchers found that on a second viewing, the animals preferentially looked at the right-hand doorway around 3 seconds before the ape burst in, demonstrating recall of locational content. The second movie allowed them to show that the apes could also remember what items were relevant to a plot.

In the first screening, a human character chose one of two adjacent weapons to launch a revenge attack on the ape 24 seconds in. Cunningly, the second screening used a slightly different version which swapped the positions of the two weapons. The animals focused their anticipatory glances on the weapon used in the first showing, not where it had been in the first showing, demonstrating that they knew what it would be used for and their expectation that the character would select it again, even though it was in a different place.

Explain what the Japanese researchers found in their experiment about apes and what the difference between their method and previous method is. When you answer the questions, do NOT copy more than FIVE consecutive words from the passage.

NOTE

Step 1	Survey
Key Words	
Signal Words	
Step 2	**Reading**
Purpose	
Pattern of Organization	
Tone	
Main Idea	
Step 3	**Summary**
지문 요약하기 (Paraphrasing)	
Step 4	**Recite**
요약문 말로 설명하기	

03 **Read the passage and follow the directions.** [4 points]

To one who stands outside the cycle of beliefs and passions which make the war seem necessary, an isolation, an almost unbearable separation from the general activity, becomes unavoidable. At the very moment when the universal disaster raises compassion in the highest degree, compassion itself compels aloofness from the impulse to self-destruction which has swept over the world. The helpless longing to save men from the ruin towards which they are hastening makes it necessary to oppose the stream, to incur hostility, to be thought unfeeling, to lose for the moment the power of winning belief. It is impossible to prevent others from feeling hostile, but it is possible to avoid any reciprocal ____________ on one's own part, by imaginative understanding and the sympathy which grows out of it. And without understanding and sympathy it is impossible to find a cure for the evil from which the world is suffering.

There are two views of the war neither of which seems to me adequate. The usual view in this country is that it is due to the wickedness of the Germans; the view of most pacifists is that it is due to the diplomatic tangle and to the ambitions of Governments. I think both these views fail to realize the extent to which war grows out of ordinary human nature. Germans, and also the men who compose Governments, are on the whole average human beings, actuated by the same passions that actuate others, not differing much from the rest of the world except in their circumstances. War is accepted by men who are neither Germans nor diplomatists with a readiness, an acquiescence in untrue and inadequate reasons, which would not be possible if any deep repugnance to war were widespread in other nations or classes. The untrue things which men believe, and the true things which they disbelieve, are an index to their impulses—not necessarily to individual impulses in each case (since beliefs are contagious), but to the general impulses of the community.

Fill in the blank with the ONE word from the passage. If necessary, change the word form. Second, describe the two conventional opinions on the war and explain why the writer does not accept those views. When you answer the questions, do NOT copy more than FIVE consecutive words from the passage.

NOTE

Step 1	Survey
Key Words	
Signal Words	
Step 2	**Reading**
Purpose	
Pattern of Organization	
Tone	
Main Idea	
Step 3	**Summary**
지문 요약하기 (Paraphrasing)	
Step 4	**Recite**
요약문 말로 설명하기	

04 **Read the passage and follow the directions.** [4 points]

Miles Davis was a ① <u>protean</u> figure in Jazz; like some musical Picasso, he mastered and then shed a series of styles throughout the course of his career. This is rare in any artist, but almost unheard of in the world of jazz, where a musician's style is usually formed extremely early, and then refined and repeated for the remainder of his or her life. Although Davis could have earned millions by continuing to play the music that had first made him famous in the 1950s, he refused to repeat himself. He consistently sought to expand his musical horizon, working with young, emerging musicians, restlessly searching for new sounds.

After cutting his teeth on the bebop jazz of the 1940s, David developed a "cooker" style and made his name in the 1950s with a five-man combo. The so-called "purists" have often claimed that ② <u>this period represents the zenith of Davis's achievement</u>. But this argument reveals more about the narrow tastes of certain critics than it does about the supposed limitations of Miles Davis. The groups Davis led in the 1960s featured a new generation of superb musicians such as Wayne Shorter and Herbie Hancok, and produced music that explored new and complex rhythmic textures.

Yet critics continued to complain. And when Davis released Bitches Brew in 1970, the jazz "purists" were horrified: His band was using electronic instruments, and its music borrowed heavily from rock rhythms and the psychedelic sound of "acid" rock. Typically, Davis ignored the storm of protest, secure in his artistic vision. Throughout the early 1970s, he continued to attract the best new players to his side. They benefited from his vast experience and mastery, and he from their youthful energy and fresh approach to the music.

According to the passage, what is the difference between Miles Davis and most jazz musicians? When you answer, you may refer to the word "protean." Second, what is the writer's take on the validity of the purists' argument "this period represents the zenith of Davis's achievement"? Write your answer in about 20 words.

NOTE

Step 1	Survey
Key Words	
Signal Words	
Step 2	**Reading**
Purpose	
Pattern of Organization	
Tone	
Main Idea	
Step 3	**Summary**
지문 요약하기 (Paraphrasing)	
Step 4	**Recite**
요약문 말로 설명하기	

05 Read the passage and follow the directions. [4 points]

How often have you called someone by a wrong name or title? Perhaps you were having a conference with your teacher and accidentally called him "Dad." All of us make these kinds of errors, and some of them get us into serious trouble! Research shows that we tend to confuse two people when we have similar relationships to both people. This explains why you may call your teacher "Dad", because both of them are male authority figures. This can also explain another common error, calling a boyfriend or girlfriend by the previous boyfriend or girlfriend's name. A supportive and intimate relationship with one person becomes momentarily mixed up with a supportive, warm, and intimate relationship with another. In contrast, people rarely make errors involving a very different type of ____________. For instance, you are unlikely to call your professor by your ex-boyfriend's name, unless perhaps you are involved in a heated intellectual argument with the professor, and heated intellectual arguments were the mainstay of your relationship with your past boyfriend. The above finding suggests that the cognitive structure of our social relations and the perceptions we hold of other people are organized in memory not only in terms of those specific individuals, but also in terms of the nature of our social relationships with them.

Fill in the blank with ONE word from the passage. Second, explain the circumstances that are prerequisite for a given person to be incorrectly addressed, according to the research above.

NOTE

Step 1	Survey
Key Words	
Signal Words	
Step 2	**Reading**
Purpose	
Pattern of Organization	
Tone	
Main Idea	
Step 3	**Summary**
지문 요약하기 (Paraphrasing)	
Step 4	**Recite**
요약문 말로 설명하기	

06 **Read the passage and follow the directions.** [4 points]

Bighorns are descended from wild Siberian sheep that crossed the Bering land bridge to North America about 100,000 years ago. These herds spread southward, diversifying and adapting to local habitats. Bighorn sheep inhabit steep, barren terrain that few other species can tolerate. Thanks to their hardiness, Bighorn sheep have long been a symbolic species. Early Native Americans carved their likenesses into rocks, and the first settlers embraced them as symbols of the rugged wilderness of the American West. At their peak, more than two million bighorns roamed the West, gracefully cavorting on rocky hillsides from California to Nebraska. But by the late 19th century, bighorn sheep were in trouble. The domestic sheep industry had taken hold in the West, and wild sheep had no immunity against diseases introduced by European livestock. As millions of domestic sheep inundated the landscape, deadly pathogens such as pneumonia decimated the bighorn population. Unregulated hunting took a toll on the few wild herds that remained. By 1940, the bighorn population had plummeted to fewer than 20,000, isolated in tiny enclaves scattered across the Western states. In recent decades, state wildlife management agencies have undertaken extensive conservation work to help bring bighorn sheep back from the brink. Much of the work focuses on capturing bighorns from successful herds and relocating them to other areas. The bighorns are carried in bags beneath the helicopter to a handling area where veterinarians examine the sheep for signs of ____________. If the sheep are healthy, they are transported to their new home. So far, more than 2,000 sheep have been successfully transplanted. This type of intensive conservation work has helped increase Nevada's bighorn population to more than 11,000, from a low of 2,000 in the mid-20th century.

Fill in the blank above with ONE word found in the passage, you may change the word form if necessary. Additionally, explain the significance the Bighorn sheep had for earlier settlers and the reason for this.

NOTE

Step 1	Survey
Key Words	
Signal Words	
Step 2	**Reading**
Purpose	
Pattern of Organization	
Tone	
Main Idea	
Step 3	**Summary**
지문 요약하기 (Paraphrasing)	
Step 4	**Recite**
요약문 말로 설명하기	

07 **Read the passage and follow the directions.** [4 points]

Some facts contradict the central dogma's cardinal maxim: that a DNA gene exclusively governs the molecular processes that give rise to a particular inherited trait. Because of their commitment to an obsolete theory, most molecular biologists operate under the assumption that DNA is the secret of life, whereas the careful observation of the hierarchy of living processes strongly suggests it is the other way around.

Why, then, has the ____________ continued to stand? To some degree the theory has been protected from criticism by a device more common to religion than science: dissent, or merely the discovery of a discordant fact, is a punishable offense, a heresy that might easily lead to professional ostracism. Much of this bias can be attributed to institutional inertia, a failure of rigor, but there are other, more insidious, reasons why molecular geneticists might be satisfied with the status quo: the central dogma has given them such a satisfying, seductively simplistic explanation of heredity.

Fill in the blank with TWO most appropriate consecutive words from the passage. Second, what is the protection of the status quo mentioned in the passage compared to?

NOTE

Step 1	Survey
Key Words	
Signal Words	
Step 2	**Reading**
Purpose	
Pattern of Organization	
Tone	
Main Idea	
Step 3	**Summary**
지문 요약하기 (Paraphrasing)	
Step 4	**Recite**
요약문 말로 설명하기	

08 **Read the passage and follow the directions.** [4 points]

In Plato's early works, the so-called Socratic dialogues, there are no indications that the search for virtue and the human good goes beyond the human realm. This changes with the growing interest in an all-encompassing metaphysical grounding of knowledge in Plato's middle dialogues that leads to the recognition of the 'Forms'—the true nature of all things, culminating in the Form of the Good as the transcendent principle of all goodness. Moral values must be based on an appropriate political order that can be maintained only by leaders with a rigorous philosophic training. Though the theory of the Forms is not confined to human values but embraces the nature of all there is, Plato at this point seems to presuppose no more than an analogy between human affairs and ____________ harmony. The late dialogues, by contrast, display a growing tendency to see a unity between the microcosm of human life and the order of the entire universe. Such holistic tendencies would seem to put the attainment of the requisite knowledge beyond human boundaries. Though Plato's late works do not display any readiness to lower the standards of knowledge as such, in his discussion of cosmic order he leaves room for conjecture and speculation, a fact that is reflected in <u>a more pragmatic treatment</u> of ethical standards and political institutions.

Choose the ONE word from the passage that best completes the blank. Then, describe what the underlined "a more pragmatic treatment" means.

NOTE

Step 1	Survey
Key Words	
Signal Words	
Step 2	**Reading**
Purpose	
Pattern of Organization	
Tone	
Main Idea	
Step 3	**Summary**
지문 요약하기 (Paraphrasing)	
Step 4	**Recite**
요약문 말로 설명하기	

09 **Read the passage and follow the directions.** [4 points]

Since the middle of the 20th century, a significant alteration has occurred in the relativity of conduct and moral. Before that, people had little doubt that there existed a gap between 'good' and 'bad', the former being coloured a dazzling white and the latter being coloured in unrelieved black. Freud and Jung and their disciples have changed all that, though. We now have learnt that nothing a person ever does is really his fault, but due to repressions and inhibitions derived from parental incompetence or undeveloped opportunities and glands.

There are some old-fashioned people like me, however, who still regard with some distrust these explanations of psycho-analysis. Being an individualist by conviction, I regard individuals as responsible for their own actions, and the relativity of ____________ responsibility inculcated by the teachings of the psycho-analyst seems to me as depressing and discouraging as the old doctrine of predestination.

In the given passage, fill in the blank with ONE word found in the passage. If necessary, change the word form. Then, state the author's opinion regarding Freud and Jung's point of view.

____

____

____

____

____

NOTE

Step 1	Survey
Key Words	
Signal Words	
Step 2	**Reading**
Purpose	
Pattern of Organization	
Tone	
Main Idea	
Step 3	**Summary**
지문 요약하기 (Paraphrasing)	
Step 4	**Recite**
요약문 말로 설명하기	

10 **Read the passage and follow the directions.** [4 points]

The Civil War represents a sort of watershed in American art. At the beginning of the rebellion, romantic images still dominated painting in general as well as battle art. During the war, however, photography and illustrated journalism emerged and placed more realistic images of war before the public at low prices. Mass-produced woodcut engravings, particularly in magazines such as Harper's and Frank Leslie's *Illustrated Newspaper*, carried drawings and sketches to large audiences. While illustrated journalism flourished during the Civil War, photography was still in its infancy. Roger Fenton, an Englishman, had pioneered war photography during the Crimean War only a few years before the firing on Fort Sumter. Several practitioners followed the troops during the Civil War, most notably Mathew Brady, perhaps the best known of all American photographers. By the end of the century, photography was well on its way to displacing hand-drawn art as the basic pictorial record of war. This emergence of war photography gave painters more latitude in selection and interpretation of subjects. They were no longer compelled to commemorate important events and turned instead to narrative painting of camp life and unfamiliar skirmishes. But the shift from memorialization of critical episodes did not mean that military art became less consequential. Freed from the necessity of depicting the sweep of major events, artists could probe more deeply the emotions and strains of combat life. The resultant narrative painting did not draw its significance from the renown of the events portrayed but rather from what it said about men at war.

Identify the media through which the public regarded the Civil War. Second, from which imagery could an understanding of the personal effects of war on the soldier be observed?

NOTE

Step 1	Survey
Key Words	
Signal Words	
Step 2	**Reading**
Purpose	
Pattern of Organization	
Tone	
Main Idea	
Step 3	**Summary**
지문 요약하기 (Paraphrasing)	
Step 4	**Recite**
요약문 말로 설명하기	

11 **Read the passage and follow the directions.** [3 points]

Why does Shylock, a Jewish loan shark in Shakespeare's play *The Merchant of Venice* turn out to be such a villain, demanding literally a pound of flesh—in effect Antonio's death—if he cannot fulfil his obligations? The answer is that Shylock is one of the many moneylenders in history to have belonged to an ethnic minority. By Shakespeare's time, Jews had been providing commercial credit in Venice for nearly a century. They did their business in front of the building once known as the Banco Rosso, which was located in a cramped ghetto some distance from the center of the city. There was a good reason why Venetian merchants had to come to the Jewish ghetto if they wanted to borrow money. For Christians, usury was a sin. Usurers had been excommunicated by the Third Lateran Council in 1179. Jews, too, were not supposed to lend at interest. But there was a convenient get-out clause in the Old Testament Book of Deuteronomy: "Unto a stranger thou mayest lend upon usury; but unto thy brother thou shalt not lend upon usury." In other words, a Jew might legitimately lend to a Christian, though not to another Jew. The price of doing so was social exclusion. In 1516, the Venetian authorities designated a special area of the city for Jews on the site of an old iron foundry which became known as the ghetto nuovo (ghetto literally means casting). There they were to be confined every night and on Christian holidays.

Based on the given passage, provide one way a Christian might loan to another legitimately.

NOTE

Step 1	Survey
Key Words	
Signal Words	
Step 2	**Reading**
Purpose	
Pattern of Organization	
Tone	
Main Idea	
Step 3	**Summary**
지문 요약하기 (Paraphrasing)	
Step 4	**Recite**
요약문 말로 설명하기	

12 **Read the passage and follow the directions.** [4 points]

Homo sapiens sapiens reached the Americas much later than they did any other landmass. The earliest confirmed human occupation in the Western Hemisphere dates to about 10,500 B.C., some forty thousand years after the settling of the Eurasian landmass and Australia. Accordingly, all human remains found so far in the Americas belong to the Homo sapiens species. We know, however, much less about the settlement of the Americas than we do about the other continents. Scholars are not certain which routes the early settlers took, when they came, or if they traveled over land or by water. Far fewer human burials have been found in the Americas, and the few that have been found were excavated with much less scientific care than in Eurasia and Africa. Many sites had been disturbed so that the original layers of earth, so valuable to archaeologists, are no longer intact. Many early sites contain no human remains at all. One theory is that humans reached America on a land bridge from Siberia. Beringia is the landmass, now below water, that connected the tip of Siberia in Russia with the northeastern corner of Alaska. Today Beringia is covered by an 80-km-wide stretch of the Bering Sea. The water in this part of the Bering Sea is shallow. As the earth experienced different periods of extended coldness, called Ice Ages, ocean water froze and covered such northern landmasses with ice. During these periods the ocean level declined and the ancient Beringia landmass emerged to form a land bridge between Russia and America.

Identify the key evidence needed to expand scholars' understanding of early human settlers of the Americas. Second, describe the problem that has occurred with gathering this key evidence so far in America.

NOTE

Step 1	Survey
Key Words	
Signal Words	
Step 2	**Reading**
Purpose	
Pattern of Organization	
Tone	
Main Idea	
Step 3	**Summary**
지문 요약하기 (Paraphrasing)	
Step 4	**Recite**
요약문 말로 설명하기	

13 **Read the passage and follow the directions.** [4 points]

Schooling is primarily a linguistic process, and language serves as an often unconscious means of evaluating and differentiating students. Inasmuch as content and disciplinary knowledge are constituted and presented through language, learning an academic subject means reading and writing texts that are organized linguistically to accomplish particular communicative purposes. In school, students are expected to use language to demonstrate what they have learned and what they think in ways that can be shared, evaluated, and further challenged or supported. But language patterns themselves are rarely the focus of attention of students and teachers. Their attention is typically on the content of the texts they read and respond to but not on the ways language construes that content. In addition, teachers' expectations for language use are seldom made explicit, and much of what is expected regarding language use in school tasks remains couched in teachers' vague admonitions to "use your own words" or to "be clear." Writing tasks are assigned without clear guidelines for students about how a particular text type is typically structured and organized. For these reasons Christie has called language the "hidden curriculum" of schooling. Judgments about students' abilities are often based on how they express their knowledge in language. The testing, counseling, and classroom interactions that inform these judgments perpetuate and maintain values that are often not made explicit. This suggests that a careful analysis of the ____________ challenges of learning is important for understanding the difficulties students face and the limitations they demonstrate in talking and writing about topics they have studied.

Choose the ONE word that best fills in the blank. Then, based on the above passage, describe the standards that teachers have that are not made explicit.

____

____

____

____

____

NOTE

Step 1	Survey
Key Words	
Signal Words	
Step 2	**Reading**
Purpose	
Pattern of Organization	
Tone	
Main Idea	
Step 3	**Summary**
지문 요약하기 (Paraphrasing)	
Step 4	**Recite**
요약문 말로 설명하기	

14 **Read the passage and follow the directions.** [4 points]

To understand why introverts and extroverts might react differently to the prospect of rewards, you have to know a little about brain structure. Our limbic system, which we share with the most primitive mammals and which Dorn calls the "old brain," is emotional and instinctive. It comprises various structures, including the amygdala, and it's highly interconnected with the nucleus accumbens, sometimes called the brain's "pleasure center." The old brain, according to Dorn, is constantly telling us, "Yes, yes, yes! Eat more, drink more, take lots of risk, go for all the gusto you can get, and above all, do not think!". The reward-seeking, pleasure-loving part of the old brain is what Dorn believes spurred people to treat their life savings like chips at the casino. We also have a "new brain" called the neocortex, which evolved many thousands of years after the limbic system. The new brain is responsible for thinking, planning, language, and decision-making—some of the very faculties that make us human. Although the new brain also plays a significant role in our emotional lives, it's the seat of rationality. Its job, according to Dorn, includes saying, "No, no, no! Don't do that, because it's dangerous, makes no sense, and is not in your best interests, or those of your family, or of society." The old brain and the new brain do work together, but not always efficiently. Sometimes they're actually in conflict, and then our decisions are a function of which one is sending out stronger signals.

In the given passage, identify the analogy used to exemplify impulsivity or sensational crisis the writer provides. Also, which of the two parts of the brain would be sending stronger signals in a speaker of three languages?

NOTE

Step 1	Survey
Key Words	
Signal Words	
Step 2	**Reading**
Purpose	
Pattern of Organization	
Tone	
Main Idea	
Step 3	**Summary**
지문 요약하기 (Paraphrasing)	
Step 4	**Recite**
요약문 말로 설명하기	

15 **Read the passage and follow the directions.** [3 points]

Corot, the most prolific and influential landscape painter of the nineteenth century, had declined an invitation to join the Impressionist exhibition, but his influence was clearly felt in many of the works shown there by artists such as Monet, Pissarro, and Renoir. Corot, like many other artists, had sketched outdoors but used his sketches to create works in the studio. These works had the finish, particularly with regard to paint handling and compositional balance, that was an integral element of academic art. The Impressionists, however, not only made sketches but also painted finished works in the open, which transformed their style by preserving the spontaneity of direct observation. They adopted colors that more accurately reflected actual visual experience and avoided using blacks and browns for shadows and modeling. As a result, their paintings emphasized color, light, and atmospheric effects. Moreover, their relatively loose and open brushwork underscored their freedom from the meticulously detailed academic manner that previously had been central to French painting.

Explain the main difference between Corot and Impressionist's paintings, according to the passage.

NOTE

Step 1	Survey
Key Words	
Signal Words	
Step 2	**Reading**
Purpose	
Pattern of Organization	
Tone	
Main Idea	
Step 3	**Summary**
지문 요약하기 (Paraphrasing)	
Step 4	**Recite**
요약문 말로 설명하기	

16 **Read the passage and follow the directions.** [4 points]

No one civilization can possibly utilize in its mores the whole potential range of human behavior. Every society, beginning with some inclination in one direction or another, carries its preference farther and farther, integrating itself more and more completely upon its chosen basis, and discarding those types of behaviors that are uncongenial. Most of those organizations of personality that seem to us more incontrovertibly abnormal have been used by different civilizations in the very foundations of their institutional life. Conversely, the most valued traits of our normal individuals have been looked on in differently organized cultures as aberrant. Normality, in short, within a very wide range, is culturally defined. The very eyes with which we see the problem are conditioned by the long traditional habits of our own society.

It is a point that has been made more often in relation to ethics than in relation to psychiatry. We do not any longer make the mistake of deriving the morality of our own locality and decade directly from the inevitable constitution of human nature. We do not elevate it to the dignity of a first principle. We recognize that ____________ differs in every society, and is a convenient term for socially approved habits. Mankind has always preferred to say, "It is morally good" rather than "It is habitual." But historically the two phrases are synonymous.

Identify the ONE word from the passage that most appropriately fills in the blank. You may change the word form if necessary. Then, write of how our society's normal behavior could be defined by differently-organized cultures.

NOTE

Step 1	Survey
Key Words	
Signal Words	
Step 2	**Reading**
Purpose	
Pattern of Organization	
Tone	
Main Idea	
Step 3	**Summary**
지문 요약하기 (Paraphrasing)	
Step 4	**Recite**
요약문 말로 설명하기	

17 **Read the passage and follow the directions.** [4 points]

Many Asian cultures are team-oriented, but not in the way that Westerners think of teams. Individuals in Asia see themselves as part of a greater whole—whether family, corporation, or community—and place tremendous value on harmony within their group. They often subordinate their own desires to the group's interests, accepting their place in its hierarchy. Western culture, by contrast, is organized around the ____________. We see ourselves as self-contained units; our destiny is to express ourselves, to follow our bliss, to be free of undue restraint, to achieve the one thing that we, and we alone, were brought into this world to do. We may be gregarious, but we don't submit to group will, or at least we don't like to think we do. We love and respect our parents, but bridle at notions like filial piety, with their implications of subordination and restraint. When we get together with others, we do so as self-contained units having fun with, competing with, standing out from, jockeying for position with, and, yes, loving, other self-contained units. It makes sense, then, that Westerners value boldness and verbal skill, traits that promote individuality, while Asians prize quiet, humility, and sensitivity, which foster group cohesion. If you live in a collective, then things will go a lot more smoothly if you behave with restraint, even submission.

In the given passage, choose the ONE most appropriate word to fill the blank. You may change the word form if necessary. Second, explain how Asians act with family in contrast to Westerners.

NOTE

Step 1	Survey
Key Words	
Signal Words	
Step 2	**Reading**
Purpose	
Pattern of Organization	
Tone	
Main Idea	
Step 3	**Summary**
지문 요약하기 (Paraphrasing)	
Step 4	**Recite**
요약문 말로 설명하기	

18 **Read the passage and follow the directions.** [4 points]

The ancient stone statues at San Agustín are among the most mysterious pre-Columbian archaeological artefacts. So far archaeologists have discovered 40 large burial mounds containing 600 likenesses of mythical animals, gods and chieftains in what is South America's largest complex of megalithic statues. Like other sites in the region, San Agustín has suffered plunder. Konrad Preuss, a German anthropologist who led the first European excavations there, shipped 35 statues that he found to a museum in Berlin, where they remain. This history has made the local inhabitants, who live from tourist visits to the site, suspicious. So it proved to be when by the national museum made a plan to take 20 of the statues to the capital, Bogotá, a ten-hour drive away, for a three-month exhibition to mark the centenary of Preuss's discovery of the site. Aware of the sensitivity of removing the statues even temporarily, anthropologists from the Colombian Institute of Anthropology held town meetings to explain the importance of allowing them to be seen by a wider public. But the locals said they worried that the objects would not return, or would be swapped for replicas. As the date for the exhibition neared, they began making demands, such as asking for a new drinking-water system for the town in exchange for letting the statues go. No deal was agreed. On the day last month when the sculptures were to travel to Bogotá, locals blockaded the road and prevented workers from loading the trucks. The museum has adopted its own form of protest. The exhibition opened, minus statues, on November 28. Light is projected where the statues would have been; guides use a virtual-reality program and tablet computers to show visitors a 3D image of what was meant to be there. The museum has taken a robust position: the opening display invites visitors to consider "the emptiness and silence that emerge when a few people claim exclusive right over our heritage, trampling the cultural liberties of all Colombians."

Describe the financial significance the statues hold for villagers. Then, explain what earlier incident might have created distrust amidst villagers as mentioned above. Do not copy more than FOUR consecutive words in your answer.

NOTE

Step 1	Survey
Key Words	
Signal Words	
Step 2	**Reading**
Purpose	
Pattern of Organization	
Tone	
Main Idea	
Step 3	**Summary**
지문 요약하기 (Paraphrasing)	
Step 4	**Recite**
요약문 말로 설명하기	

19 **Read the passage and follow the directions.** [4 points]

> The Englishmen who were quickly populating the Atlantic seaboard from the Carolinas to New England had no monopoly on the New World. French and Dutch explorers had also been busy, and both nations were carving out separate territories in North America. The Dutch founded New Netherlands in the Hudson Valley of present-day New York State, basing their claims upon the exploration of Henry Hudson in 1609.
>
> An Englishman, Hudson was hired by a Dutch company that wanted to find the Northeast Passage, the sea route to China along the northern rim of Asia. In 1609, Hudson set off instead, aboard the Half Moon, for the northwest alternative. Sailing down the Atlantic coast, he entered Chesapeake Bay before making a U-turn and heading back north to explore the Hudson River as far upriver as Albany. Noting the absence of tides, he correctly assumed that this route did not lead to the Pacific.
>
> England was flexing its new muscles in the early 1600s, but it was the Dutch who had become the true world power in maritime matters by building the world's largest merchant marine fleet. There was literally not a place in the known world of that day in which the Dutch did not have a hand in matters. Amsterdam had become the busiest and richest city in the European world. In 1621, the Dutch West India Company was formed with the aim of taking over trade between Europe and the New World, and the Dutch soon took from the Portuguese control of the lucrative slave and sugar trading outpost in 1624. Two years later, the trading village of New Amsterdam, later to be renamed New York, was established at the mouth of the Hudson. The Dutch West India Company did more than trade and set up colonies. In 1628, the Dutch Admiral Piet Hein captured a Spanish treasure fleet, pirating away enough silver to provide company shareholders with a 75-percent dividend.

Identify the major error in European navigation in the given passage. Second, identify the most powerful European force in the Americas in the seventeenth century.

NOTE

Step 1	Survey
Key Words	
Signal Words	
Step 2	Reading
Purpose	
Pattern of Organization	
Tone	
Main Idea	
Step 3	Summary
지문 요약하기 (Paraphrasing)	
Step 4	Recite
요약문 말로 설명하기	

20 **Read the passage and follow the directions.** [4 points]

There are today about 190 million people in the world who live in a country other than the one in which they were born—nearly 60 percent of them are in rich countries (about 36 million in Europe and 38 million in the United States). People migrate primarily for economic reasons, but some do so to escape political and religious oppression. The 38 million foreign-born people who live in the United States represent 12.6 percent of the U.S. population. Of these, 11 million, or nearly 30 percent, entered the nation illegally. Most nations impose restrictions on immigration to reduce the inflow of low-skilled people (while often encouraging the immigration of highly skilled and technical people). Migration is generally more restricted and regulated than the international flow of goods, services and capital.

In general, ____________ flows more freely across national boundaries than people. Financial or portfolio capital (bank loans and bonds) generally move to nations and markets where interest rates are higher, and foreign direct investments in plants and firms flow to nations where expected profits are higher. This leads to more efficient use of capital and generally benefits both lenders and borrowers. During the 1970s, Middle Eastern nations deposited a great deal of their huge earnings from petroleum exports in New York and London banks, which then lent (recycled) them to Latin American and Asian governments and corporations. During the 1980s, Japan invested a large chunk of its huge export earnings in financial assets and real estate and set up corporate subsidiaries in the United States. Since the mid-1980s, the United States has become an increasingly large net borrower from the rest of the world to cover its excess of spending over production. Global banks established branches in major international monetary centers around the world, nearly $3 trillion of foreign currencies are exchanged each day by around-the-clock trading in world financial centers, and newly-established sovereign funds (financial institutions owned by Middle Eastern petroleum exporting nations, Singapore, China, Russia, and Brazil) are making huge investments of all kinds all over the world. Financial markets are globalized as never before. The downside is that when a financial crisis starts in one country it quickly spreads to others.

Fill in the blank with the ONE most appropriate word from the passage. Second, state the reason that can be inferred that the United States has drawn a large immigrant population.

NOTE

Step 1	Survey
Key Words	
Signal Words	
Step 2	**Reading**
Purpose	
Pattern of Organization	
Tone	
Main Idea	
Step 3	**Summary**
지문 요약하기 (Paraphrasing)	
Step 4	**Recite**
요약문 말로 설명하기	

21 **Read the passage and follow the directions.** [4 points]

A very large number of people cease when quite young to add anything to a limited stock of judgments. After a certain age, say 25, they consider that their education finished. It is perhaps natural that having passed through that painful and boring process, expressly called education, they should suppose it over and think that they are equipped for life to label every event as it occurs and drop it into its given pigeonhole. But one who has a label ready for everything does not bother to observe any more, even such ordinary happenings as he had observed for himself, with attention, before he went to school. He merely acts and reacts. For people who have stopped noticing, the only possible new or renewed experience, and therefore new knowledge, is from a work of art. Because that is the only kind of experience which they are prepared to receive on its own terms, they will come out from their shells and expose themselves to music, to a play, to a book, because it is the accepted method of enjoying <u>such things</u>. True, even to plays and books they may bring artistic prejudices which prevent them from seeing that play or comprehending that book. Their artistic sensibilities may be as crusted over as their minds. But it is part of an artist's job to break crusts, or let us say rather that artists who work for the public and not merely for themselves are interested in breaking crusts because they want to communicate their intuitions.

Describe to what the underlined "such things" refer. Second, complete the following sentence by filling in the blank with the TWO most appropriate consecutive words from the passage.

The writer sees the artist as a man charged with the responsibility for ____________ of people's routinized thought patterns.

NOTE

Step 1	Survey
Key Words	
Signal Words	
Step 2	**Reading**
Purpose	
Pattern of Organization	
Tone	
Main Idea	
Step 3	**Summary**
지문 요약하기 (Paraphrasing)	
Step 4	**Recite**
요약문 말로 설명하기	

22 **Read the passage and follow the directions.** [4 points]

An auction is usually advertised beforehand with full particulars of the articles to be sold and where and when they can be viewed by prospective buyers. If the advertisement cannot give full details, catalogues are printed, and each group of goods to be sold together, called a "lot", is usually given a number. The auctioneer need not begin with Lot 1 and continue in numerical order. He may wait until he registers the fact that certain dealers are in the room and then produce the lots they are likely to be interested in. The auctioneer's services are paid for in the form of a percentage of the price the goods are sold for. The auctioneer therefore has a direct interest in pushing up the bidding as high as possible. The auctioneer must know fairly accurately the current market values of the goods he is selling, and he should be acquainted with regular buyers of such goods. He will not waste time by starting the bidding too ______①______. He will also play on the rivalries among his buyers and succeed in getting a high price by encouraging two business competitors to bid against each other. It is largely on his advice that a seller will fix a "reserve" price, that is, a price below which the goods cannot be sold. Even the best auctioneers, however, find it difficult to stop a ② "knock-out" whereby dealers illegally arrange beforehand not to bid against each other, but nominate one of themselves as the only bidder, in the hope of buying goods at extremely low prices. If such a knock-out comes off, the real auction sale takes place privately afterwards among the dealers.

Fill in the blank with the ONE most appropriate word from the passage. Second, explain why a "knock-out" is arranged.

NOTE

Step 1	Survey
Key Words	
Signal Words	
Step 2	**Reading**
Purpose	
Pattern of Organization	
Tone	
Main Idea	
Step 3	**Summary**
지문 요약하기 (Paraphrasing)	
Step 4	**Recite**
요약문 말로 설명하기	

23 **Read the passage and follow the directions.** [4 points]

We go see a horror movie to reestablish our feelings of essential normality; the horror movie is innately conventional. It urges us to put away our more civilized and adult penchant for analysis and to become children again, seeing things in pure blacks and whites. And we go to have fun. This is where the ground starts to slope away, because this is a very peculiar sort of fun. The fun comes from seeing others menaced—sometimes killed. A critic has suggested that the horror film has become the modern version of the public ______①______. The potential lyncher is in almost all of us, and every now and then, he has to be let loose. Our emotions and our fears form their own body, and we recognize that it demands its own exercise to maintain proper muscle tone. Certain of these emotional muscles are accepted, even exalted, in civilized society. Love, friendship, loyalty, kindness—these are the emotions that we applaud. When we exhibit these emotions, society showers us with positive reinforcement. But anticivilization emotions don't go away, and they demand periodic exercise. The horror movie has a dirty job to do. It deliberately appeals to all that is worst in us. It is morbidity unchained, our most abject instincts set free, our nastiest fantasies realized. The most aggressive of horror films lifts a trapdoor in the civilized forebrain and throws a basket of raw meat to the hungry alligators swimming around in that subterranean river beneath. It keeps them from getting out. It keeps ② <u>them</u> down there and me up here.

Fill in blank ① with ONE word from the passage. If necessary, change the word from. Second, identify to what the underlined "them" refers.

NOTE

Step 1	Survey
Key Words	
Signal Words	
Step 2	**Reading**
Purpose	
Pattern of Organization	
Tone	
Main Idea	
Step 3	**Summary**
지문 요약하기 (Paraphrasing)	
Step 4	**Recite**
요약문 말로 설명하기	

24 **Read the passage and follow the directions.** [4 points]

> Traditional research has confronted only Mexican and United States interpretations of Mexican-American culture. Now we must also examine the culture as we Mexican-Americans have experienced it, passing from a sovereign people to compatriots with newly arriving settlers to, finally, a conquered people—<u>a charter minority on our own land</u>. When the Spanish first came to Mexico, they intermarried with and absorbed the culture of the indigenous Indians. This policy of colonization through acculturation was continued when Mexico acquired Texas in the early 1800s and brought the indigenous Indians into Mexican life and government. In the 1820s, United States citizens migrated to Texas, attracted by land suitable for cotton. As their numbers became more substantial, their policy of acquiring land by subduing native populations began to dominate. The two ideologies clashed repeatedly, culminating in a military conflict that led to victory for the United States. Thus, suddenly deprived of our parent culture, we had to evolve uniquely Mexican-American modes of thought and action in order to survive.

Explain why the author employs the phrase "a charter minority on our own land" in the first paragraph. Second, describe the writer's primary purpose in the passage.

NOTE

Step 1	Survey
Key Words	
Signal Words	
Step 2	**Reading**
Purpose	
Pattern of Organization	
Tone	
Main Idea	
Step 3	**Summary**
지문 요약하기 (Paraphrasing)	
Step 4	**Recite**
요약문 말로 설명하기	

유희태 일반영어 ②
2S2R 유형

초판 1쇄 2014년 3월 13일
2쇄 2014년 3월 29일
2판 1쇄 2015년 2월 17일
2쇄 2015년 2월 23일
3쇄 2016년 2월 25일
3판 1쇄 2017년 3월 10일
2쇄 2018년 2월 20일
3쇄 2018년 12월 15일
4판 1쇄 2020년 2월 10일
2쇄 2020년 12월 10일
5판 1쇄 2022년 1월 10일
2쇄 2023년 1월 5일
3쇄 2024년 9월 5일

저자와의
협의하에
인지생략

저자 유희태 **발행인** 박 용 **발행처** (주)박문각출판
표지디자인 박문각 디자인팀
등록 2015. 4. 29. 제2015-000104호
주소 06654 서울시 서초구 효령로 283 서경 B/D
팩스 (02) 584-2927
전화 교재 문의 (02) 6466-7202 동영상 문의 (02) 6466-7201

정 가 31,000원 (분권 포함)
ISBN 979-11-6704-326-9
ISBN 979-11-6704-325-2(세트)